Real, Raw, and Respectful Talk about Suicide

EYES ABOVE THE Water

Bill Vassilopoulos

EYES ABOVE THE WATER: REAL, RAW AND RESPECTFUL TALK ABOUT SUICIDE

This is a work of creative nonfiction. The events are portrayed to the best of Bill Vassilopoulos's memory. While all the stories in this book are true, some names and identifying details have been changed to protect the privacy of the people involved.

This book is not intended as a substitute for the medical advice of physicians. The reader should regularly consult a physician in matters relating to his/her health and particularly with respect to any symptoms that may require diagnosis or medical attention.

ISBN: 978-1-4866-1624-4
eBook ISBN: 978-1-4866-1625-1

Word Alive Press
119 De Baets Street Winnipeg, MB R2J 3R9
www.wordalivepress.ca

Cataloguing in Publication information can be obtained from Library and Archives Canada.

This book is dedicated to all the frontliners,
people who are left behind still grieving, and courageous
people who have been interviewed for this book.
Together, we are making a difference.

FOREWORD

BILL VASSILOPOULOS IS keenly aware of the elephant in the room—the global mental health and suicide crisis that many of us avoid talking about. The global rise in mental health struggles and illnesses is prompting our organizations, schools, and communities to prioritize psychological wellbeing alongside physical health and safety. Laws now emphasize society's duty to protect and accommodate the psychological needs of citizens, making it imperative for everyone to take meaningful action. More needs to be done.

Much-needed efforts are underway to educate frontliners in psychological safety protocols to ensure mental wellness and resilience in workplaces, educational institutions, and recreational spaces. Normalizing attitudes towards mental health struggles and suicidal ideation is crucial in proactively safeguarding the brain health of individuals. More needs to be done.

Bill Vassilopoulos is a survivor of suicide. He realizes all too well that, instead of merely discussing mental health issues, society must engage in clear, honest, and open conversations to find effective solutions. This is why Bill's book is so important and timely. People need to stop just talking about mental health and suicide; they need to share openly and candidly. The stories shared by real people in this book demonstrate this type of candidness. Understanding the impact of day-to-day stress, trauma, loss, and grief on psychological health is vital in terms of saving lives. Society is witnessing increased risks of psychological injuries, mental health problems, substance abuse, and suicide, further exacerbated by the pandemic. Hence, a sustainable strategy for psychological safety is essential. More needs to be done.

Just as people are trained in physical first aid, citizens need training to be ready, willing, and able to offer care in psychological and suicide first aid. I have had the honor and pleasure of working with Bill for over a decade now, speaking, training and advocating on this topic. Our approach complements existing wellness programs and specialized treatment services, equipping learners to assist at-risk individuals, ensure their safety, and connect them to support systems. More needs to be done.

Furthermore, empowering our leaders is crucial in order to cultivate respectful environments that encourage positive interactions, collaboration, and interpersonal risk-taking while protecting individuals from daily stress and psychological injury. Social and emotional intelligence training helps improve team dynamics and fosters harmony.

More than ever, leaders must be equipped to inspire their teams towards a shift from toxic to nurturing cultures. Recognizing how socioemotional dynamics influence the outcome for mental health is key. By motivating teams to perform better, leaders can create networks of psychological safety. Bill and I have been working tirelessly with leaders and emerging leaders to equip them with skills, behaviors, and attitudes that help people to create more nurturing culture wherever we work, learn, and play.

To summarize, the focus on mental health and suicide is increasing globally, demanding action and open discussions to find solutions. This book models the normalization of the conversation around the difficult topic of suicide. Education, awareness, and proactive measures are essential in terms of safeguarding people's psychological wellbeing, protecting life, and fostering healthier and more supportive environments in workplaces, schools, and communities. Empowered citizens play a pivotal role in driving positive change and forming networks of psychological safety on planet earth. To do this, we all need to talk about problems and solutions in this space with one hundred percent trust, respect, and honesty.

Bill Vassilopoulos knows this and is a champion for the cause. More needs to be done.

—Demetre Balaktsis
master trainer, keynote speaker, and advocate
Applied Suicide Intervention Skills Trainer

INTRODUCTION
Bystanders at the Lake

THE COLD, CRISP lake surrounded me as I dreamt one night, alone and disoriented. The darkness and isolation were overwhelming, and every tiny sound above the water amplified my anxiety. My body trembled uncontrollably and my teeth chattered from the cold. As I struggled to breathe, I found myself surrounded by invisible walls, unable to see or hear anyone. Panic consumed me, my heart raced, and an intense headache added to my distress. The waves grew larger, and with every breath more freezing water filled my lungs. I coughed and gasped for air, but my strength was fading.

Finally, I succumbed to the depths, my eyes no longer above the water…

When I woke up on Saturday, December 12, 2022, around 5:00 a.m., I was still shaking under my blanket and heavy comforter. My body ached from the flu I had been battling for the past five days. Desperate for comfort, I called out for my wife, Trudy, who had sought refuge in our daughter's room to avoid catching my illness.

As she entered, she saw me struggling to catch my breath. I felt utterly helpless, trying to calm myself but unable to find relief. My burning lungs and disoriented mind made me feel surrounded by a haze of chaos. Though I tried to sit up, my body refused to cooperate.

Exhaustion overtook me and my brain drifted into memory, taking me back to when I was eight years old in 1978. On an early summer day marked by strong winds blowing through Birds Hill Provincial Park in Manitoba, I found myself at a manmade lake accompanied by my little brother George and older cousin Demetre, along with his own little brother George. We were amused by the coincidental presence of these two Greek cousins with the same name. Our outing was courtesy of Uncle Christo and Aunt Maria, who had brought us to the park.

While the two Georges ventured to the other side of the lake, I chose solitude. In fact, I yearned for a moment alone, since the lake was crowded. With Demetre enjoying the water nearby, my attention was drawn to the Georges, near the shore, by the bulrushes. At first they seemed to be laughing and having fun. But then their laughter turned into cries of distress.

Confused and concerned, I turned to Demetre, who was about forty feet away from our brothers. I yelled to him and waved, desperate to catch his attention, but he was oblivious, staring back in incomprehension. Feeling powerless, I kept shouting that the boys were in trouble and time seemed to pass in slow motion. I struggled through the water to reach them, but the waves grew stronger. My eyes remained above the waterline as I took in the chaotic scene. All other sounds faded, leaving only the urgent need to rescue the boys.

After what felt like an eternity, Demetre and a teenage girl reached the Georges and saved them. Relief washed over me as the sound of life returned to the lake.

But questions lingered in my young mind. Why had it taken so long for me to reach them? Why had I felt so weak and powerless?

And why hadn't more people stepped in to help? In a park full of people, everyone had been reduced to bystanders, shivering and staring at each other.

The impact of that event was yet to reveal its significance, but it would come to shape our young lives in ways we couldn't yet comprehend.

"Billy? Billy, are you all right?"

Trudy's voice sounded distant as I struggled to wake up from a series of unsettling dreams.

"I had a bad dream," I groggily replied. "And then I had another bad dream."

Concerned for my health, my wife checked my forehead, realizing that I wasn't getting any better. Lethargy had taken over and I felt unrelenting exhaustion.

"I need my laptop," I told her, my thoughts focused on finishing my book.

Perplexed, Trudy brought me my laptop and placed it on my desk. My commitment to completing my book project was unwavering, but my physical condition was far from ideal. Weighing two hundred ninety-five pounds and experiencing various health issues, I had been struggling since my father's passing in September 2020. The grief and depression had led me to rely on food for solace, resulting in obesity. Simple tasks like tying my shoes had become nearly impossible without feeling faint.

I felt determined to proceed and settled into my office chair, excited to delve back into the work. The brightness of the laptop screen was momentarily blinding, but I pressed on, searching for all the interviews and documents I had collected. I hadn't realized how much time had passed since I'd conducted my first interview in November 2017. The last one had been in November 2020, only about a month after my father's death.

Although I lacked credentials, since I was neither a professional journalist nor a suicidology expert, my motivation stemmed from being a survivor of suicide, a caring husband, a devoted father, and a proud grandfather. I yearned to live in a world free from the scourge of suicide, understanding that it couldn't be achieved alone. I needed help.

Nearly forty-five years after that near-drowning incident at Birds Hill Park, Demetre and I joined forces by becoming trainers at suicide intervention workshops. Our certification came through Living Works Education in Calgary, complemented by qualifications as Red Cross-certified psychological first aid instructors.

Through video conferences, we advocated for ASIST (Applied Suicide Intervention Skills Trailing) throughout Manitoba, reaching nonprofit organizations, local government leaders, healthcare and medical professionals, crisis hotline workers, military personnel, schools, EMS departments, firefighters, police officers, counselors, mental health workers, churches, and anyone else eager to address the issue of suicide. I was humbled to have been called upon to address suicide-related challenges in my own community.

People often wondered why we cared so deeply about suicide. The answer was simple: Demetre and I were driven by our desire to see this devastating problem eradicated.

In 2015, I launched my mission in my hometown of Landmark, Manitoba, intending to expand my training efforts across the province and throughout Canada. Armed with experience and commitment, I decided to conduct interviews and write about this sensitive subject. And that's precisely what I've done.

So what is suicide? I'm often asked this question, and it makes me wonder how others perceive this complex issue. My clinical response is that suicide is the result of an unintentional and intense mental health illness that leads people to experience overwhelmingly negative emotions and develop a bleak outlook on life. From a belief that they can no longer endure or manage their suffering, taking their own life comes to seem like the only possible escape.

Over the course of my adult life, I've been deeply engaged on the topic of suicide and in this book I hope to shed some clarity. People often pose a series of common questions:

1. Why do you care about suicide, and what do you hope to gain?
2. What are your thoughts on medical assistance in dying (or medical aid in dying, MAiD)?
3. At what age did you discover that you were a first responder?

I've pondered these questions extensively while striving to provide honest and insightful answers throughout this book.

Suicide profoundly impacts many groups. When I embarked on this journey, I sought out influential frontline workers to learn, and share, their perspectives. I wanted people to find their voices and stop trying to brush suicide under the proverbial rug.

We are all impacted by suicide in one way or another. For every suicide attempt or loss, according to reports, eight to eleven people are impacted by that decision. The numbers are larger when a famous person dies by suicide.

Though I couldn't interview representatives from every field, I have aimed to explore the attitudes and hearts of those I could reach, understanding how suicide might touch them in their personal lives and professions. My interviews include individuals from diverse backgrounds: an outpatient coordinator at a mental health centre, a retired registered nurse, provincial politicians, a school division superintendent, a farm journalist and broadcaster, a pastor, an advanced care paramedic, a former chief of the Winnipeg Police Service, a licensed funeral director, and a high school guidance counsellor.

Through these interviews, I seek to understand how they respond to those struggling with mental health and suicidal thoughts, and whether they actively work towards helping those affected. I ask about how often they encounter individuals contemplating suicide, their protocol for responding to such disclosures, the challenges their professions face in addressing suicide, and their perception of the effectiveness of their profession and society in handling the issue.

Most of these interviews were conducted before the COVID-19 lockdowns, using recordings from my phone. All participants offered their time and insights generously and voluntarily, without compensation. Looking forward, I plan to explore the effects of the COVID-19 lockdowns on mental health and suicide rates.

As I continue my journey, my mission remains clear: to promote awareness, understanding, and compassion in the fight against suicide. This book is about sharing stories, learning, and working together to combat this devastating problem in our families, communities, and society as a whole.

CHAPTER ONE

Crying Wolf

ON A CLOUDY and damp November day in 2017, I had the opportunity to interview Pat Smith, an outpatient coordinator at a reputable mental health centre in Winkler, Manitoba and private contractor for mental health crisis services in the Southern Health-Sante Sud health region. Pat's experience in the mental health field led me to seek his insight, especially regarding suicide, as he has assisted those struggling with both mental health and addictions.

Nervous but eager to learn, I arrived with coffees in hand, only to clumsily spill one on Pat's coffee table. After a friendly handshake, the interview commenced in his clean, quiet, and organized office.

As I sat across from Pat, I asked, "In your experience in this field with mental health, how often do you have people disclose they are contemplating suicide?"

"I'm going to focus mostly on my job as a contractor, because my job as an outpatient nursing coordinator is more administrative," he replied. "So I don't often have a lot of patient contact in that job. But I read referral letters from family physicians who say that suicidal thoughts are often mentioned. In my job as a contractor, or even the last five years that I was the emergency mental health nurse at the ER, I would say more often than not, conservatively, that eighty percent of the people I see in that capacity express suicidal thoughts. Now, most of that is because I ask directly about it every time I see a patient. It's part of my assessment. Would they spontaneously have talked about it? I don't know. Sometimes that's their entrance complaint, so it's right there off the hop. But it's just always a part of my assessment. So conservatively, seventy-five to eighty percent have thought about it and are possibly thinking about it currently."

I nodded, taking in his perspective. "And what is your protocol when somebody discloses. How do you respond to a suicidal person?"

"My protocol, basically, is more a question of how I do a proper safety assessment. So if somebody discloses that they're suicidal, I have a series of questions I ask them. That is part of the risk assessment I do. Everything depends on what the answers to those questions are. Some people come in who have been thinking about suicide for ten years. Their thoughts really haven't changed. They've never acted on them, so there's not much protocol after that. We talk about it. We talk about what the safety net could be for them.

"But if somebody is actively suicidal, if they have a plan or they feel unsafe to go home, there's a more specific protocol at that point. Generally, if I feel at the end of that conversation with somebody that they're at risk to harm themselves, like in an emergency room setting, I have to report that to the doctor and make a determination. Does this person need to be admitted for safety reasons? And that can range from a mental health facility to a crisis unit, to going home with family, having somebody watch them. Sometimes a family tells me the person is suicidal and isn't disclosing it. That changes the picture a little bit."

"If a person doesn't tell you directly that they're suicidal, what ends up happening in those situations?" I asked.

"When they don't directly tell me, but the family is telling me? That happens often, with the family. Or the police bringing them in will say they've threatened multiple times. 'I came in. They had a rope. They denied they were going to hang themselves, but all the signs were there.' Usually that's more significant for me.

"I get a lot of patients who throw it out there that they're suicidal. That is easier to work with than somebody who comes in and denies it. Because if they're denying it, they're more at risk. Generally what I do is I tell them that their family is concerned, or the police are concerned, because of this or that. But how do I respond to this, in the end, if somebody adamantly denies they're suicidal? I can't do much under the Mental Health Act. My hands are tied at that point."

"What are the biggest challenges that your profession faces when it comes to suicide?" I asked.

"Well, I would say cynicism, actually," he said. "Because cynicism and burnout really create a bit of a lack of empathy. But at the same time, there are so many patients. There's such a revolving door—in the ERs, in particular—of people who are constantly threatening suicide and using it as a currency. You start to get cynical about it. That's when it's like the boy who cried wolf, right? When somebody comes in who's really suicidal, you have this tainted view, or this cynical underlay to your assessments. So for me, after doing this for so long, that would be the thing that probably clouds me at times.

"The other barrier would just be access. Like, there are only so many mental health beds in Manitoba, which is not very many. I can have somebody who is suicidal, who I think is at risk, and there's no bed available for them. That would be a barrier. It doesn't happen very often, but it does happen. Then there's ease of access. So you might have somebody who is suicidal, but they're not imminently thinking of doing it, even though the risk is there. They think about it and those thoughts are there and they're getting more intense. Maybe this isn't someone you'd admit to a mental health facility, but they're also not somebody you'd send home with no other supports in place. What do you do? Everything has a waitlist. So you wonder, do they need therapy? Yes, but there's a six-month waitlist. Do they need a crisis unit? Yes, but they'll be sent home in four days. So it's just access most of the time, and the timing of it."

"In your opinion, how effective is your profession in responding to people who are suicidal, or to people bereaved by suicide loss?"

"I think those are separate answers. For people who are suicidal, I think our profession is fairly good at that initial contact, setting up the safety net, and doing the assessment. I don't think that piece is a problem. It's the next step that often is. My profession is not at fault, but the government resources just aren't there.

"For the second question, those affected by suicide... resources are very slim. For instance, in the Southern Health region, there are no support groups for families bereaved by suicide. We just had a family whose young teenager completed suicide and there's nothing in the region to help support them, which is terrible. In Winnipeg, I think there are two support groups for families bereaved by suicide. So I don't think we're doing a good enough job, especially with the rates of suicide. And if you go into Indigenous communities, there is even less support, even though their suicide rates are through the roof."

"Some reports say that suicide is twenty-five times higher for those communities," I noted.

"I don't doubt that for a second."

"So in your opinion, how effective do you think our society is at dealing with suicide?"

"'Dealing' is a hard word. I think society is becoming more and more aware of it, and probably social media is helping a lot in that area. People aren't as ignorant about it. So I guess, as a general umbrella, people are becoming more and more aware and in tune with mental illness. I think the stigma is getting less, and surprisingly that's only been the case in the last few years. Mental illness and suicidal thoughts are very closely tied, so the more we become open to talking about mental illness as a society, the more we'll talk about suicide as well."

"What are we doing right and what are we doing wrong?"

"Well, I think what we're doing right is talking about it and then having big organizations, like Bell, encourage the conversation. It's becoming more and more something you just see every day. That right away lessens the stigma, you know. I think it's one thing to talk about things, though, and a whole other thing to start getting involved and advocating and maybe developing more community organizations. In that way, I think we could probably grow a lot.

"One area where we could do a lot more work is in peer support for people who struggle with suicide, and for people who work with them. I think this is very weak in Manitoba. I've attended a few conferences in the United States and their peer support network is massive. So if you are suicidal, you go to the ER and you don't have to wait alone; a peer will come and wait with you. It's in place here, but I certainly think we could do a lot more. I think it's a win-win for both parties in that case because the person who is suicidal has someone who's been there and the person who is the peer is able to share their experience and grow a lot too."

"What are we doing wrong?"

"That was sort of the answer to both. So much is left up to government resources, which is a difficult position to be in."

"What could be done about how we deal with the problem of suicide?"

"I don't know. I don't think it's a simplistic answer. But again, it boils down to money, resources, and just talking about it. I think we're doing a really good job in schools. I think that piece has really improved. For example, WE Day, where they actively talk about that kind of thing. And guidance counselors are much more aware, and more clinically capable of managing it when it happens. I think we have more crisis debriefing going on than we used to, so all that is good. But it's the tip of the iceberg—because as much as we're doing, the problem is growing probably exponentially."

"How big do you think the suicide crisis is?"

"I don't know. I think it's huge in Indigenous communities, from my experience. One of the basic problems I see is the disintegration of the family unit. I think kids aren't learning coping skills anymore. Then they're hearing about self-harm. It has to do with a pack mentality. Kids are seeing other kids self-harming or threatening suicide. It's on social media. So it's a double-edged sword, because I think families aren't teaching coping skills. Then kids are exposed to this stuff more and more. The number of youth in the suicidal realm is growing, threatening suicide, but they're not necessarily completing suicide. I see those as very different things. I don't think completed suicide is a massive problem outside of Indigenous communities, but the use of self-harm and threatening suicide is growing."

"Almost like a copycat syndrome?"

"For teens especially, yeah. Girls in particular."

"Has suicide impacted you in any way in your own life?"

"I have been suicidal probably twice in my lifetime. I think most people experience suicidal thoughts at some point. Probably more do than don't. When I was seventeen, my girlfriend broke up with me. As a typical teenage boy, I thought that was the end of the world for me. I remember driving 140 or 150 kilometers per hour on a dark highway and closing my eyes and taking my hands off the wheel. I thought, 'I don't care what happens. Let's see where the dice fall.' And I stayed on the highway. I kind of grabbed the wheel and gave my head a shake. But I honestly thought that was the end of my life.

"Then, about five years ago, I went through a significant depression. I remember feeling, like, if I died today that would be just great, you know? I had kids, so I never went to the point of planning it. I had people who loved me who were always protective, but I would have welcomed death had it come. Is that suicidal? Was it more a wish to die? Are they the same? I don't know."

"Do you know anyone in your family, circle of friends, colleagues, or community who has attempted or died by suicide?"

"Yes on both. Someone very close to me became suicidal. Well, they struggled with self-harm for a long time, but they were suicidal to the point where I took them to the ER. They've also tried to kill themselves by drug overdose. So it's been pretty close to home for me."

"How does this make you feel, though? Some people feel like they've failed somehow, that they didn't give that person the tools of life."

"I don't think I felt that in particular. I work in the system, and I've also tried to access the system, especially for people close to me. It was an extremely frustrating experience. Again, it goes back to access. I heard at one point, 'You know the system, you work in it, and look how hard it is for us to get help.' Imagine the average person who doesn't have knowledge of the supports, or maybe they don't have the cognitive ability, whatever you want to call it. How hard is it for those people to get the help they need? So many people say this to me, and it's actually true. I don't argue with them. 'What is it going to take for me to get help? Do I actually have to try to kill myself?' And sometimes, yes, that's true. I hate to say it, as a health professional, but that's the reality. It's all a triage system, where the sickest of the sick are getting help, but that leaves out the seventy-five percent of people who really do need help. Resources go to the top twenty-five percent, right?"

"How have you dealt with those feelings?"

"Like, for my own feelings? I have the advantage, I guess, of knowing a lot about depression. I can cognitively say to myself, 'This will pass. Today is not a picture of your life.' I can even say to myself, 'Look around you. You have this, you have this, you have this…' I can sort of self-talk myself through it, because I do have the skills to do that. Sometimes people who are very depressed, even though they may have those skills, get lost in the moment. But me, that's how I dealt with it.

"In the case of the person I mentioned who was close to me, it's taken a lot of years of working in terms of boundaries and realizing what I can and can't do. For a lot of it, I have to take my hands off the situation. I can guide them, I can lead them, I can show them the resources that are out there, but in the end they've got to grab it. Like, I can give you all the resources in the world, but in the end you're sitting there and you're the one who has to pick up the phone and make the choices. For me, I guess it's about taking my hands off, control-wise, and loving and guiding people... giving them a safe place to fall."

As he spoke, I kept thinking about how incredibly hard this must be for someone in the system, not being able to make things happen even for those close to them.

I continued with my next question. "What else would you like to share on the topic of suicide?"

"I guess this would be a clinical perspective, but I think it's really important. I feel the media skews a lot of things through their reports about patients, impatient ones, who leave and end up harming themselves. A large majority of mental health patients have personality disorders. That really plays into self-harm and threats of suicide, which I'm differentiating from suicide attempts. There's a book called *Half in Love with Death* by Joel Paris.[1] It's a read I would recommend for anybody. The book talks about people with personality disorders, describing them as those who become half in love with death and the rush they get from it, as well as the help, the secondary gain, they get from it. This is a huge part of what's coming through the doors.

---

[1] Joel Paris, *Half in Love with Death: Managing the Chronically Suicidal Patient* (Milton Park, UK: Routledge, 2006).

And I'm not saying these people don't need help, because absolutely they do. It's a long-range therapy issue that they're often not able to access the kind of help they need. This gets skewed when you look at the whole. Just that piece, I think, is important from my clinical perspective. I would differentiate them from those who are really in a significant clinical depression."

"And my final question: what would you like to know more about in terms of suicide?"

"I'd like to know less about it. That's an honest answer! I've had a lot of grief in my life and I face this all the time in my job. So I'd like to know less about suicide. I'm not saying I'd like to be more ignorant about it, obviously, but I sure wish it wasn't crossing my path as much as it is."

As the interview drew to a close, I had a nagging thought that I was forgetting something.

"Before we started this interview, I think you mentioned how many years you've been in the field of mental health. I think you said twenty-five years?"

"Yeah. High-intensity stuff! I've seen lots of suicide deaths, lots of grieving families, lots of violence, and lots of repeat people who are consuming the system and the dollars even though they aren't significantly suicidal. So there's the cynicism. I would say that I see a really hurting society out there, and the social problems are getting bigger. The resources aren't growing with that and our capacity to support people isn't where it should be. It's a little bit like banging your head against the wall."

"It's almost like we need a Suicide Anonymous place now."

"Absolutely, that's a great idea. It would be a pretty dark group to go to, but I think it could be useful, right?" he said. "Obviously a barrier would be funding to put into places like that. Those groups are self-supported, aren't they? They're often driven by people. It could be just like starting a twelve-step group without funding, right?"

He paused and then continued with some additional thoughts.

"I think one of the biggest things we could do would be offering more CBT, cognitive behavior therapy, which is one of the best types of therapy for people who are chronically suicidal or self-harming. The other would be DBT, dialectical behavior therapy. Marsha Linehan is the one who started dialectical behavior therapy and it's being offered more and more, but it's a year-long therapy commitment and it's intense. However, it's super effective. People who are chronically suicidal say that this has got them through it and sustains them. So yeah, we could do more of that in self-help group settings."

I stood up to shake Pat's hand. For me, the interview had flown by very fast.

When I left the building and jumped into the car with my wife, Trudy asked me how the interview had gone. My head was swirling with all the good information I'd gathered, but I also felt like I wanted to have another interview with Pat. At the time, I was working with people with intellectual challenges and behavioral complexities, and I now wanted to ask how he could handle suicide intervention with the kind of people I supported.

And so I called Pat the next day and scheduled a follow-up interview.

Three weeks later, I was back at Pat's office. This time I didn't bring coffee to spill on his nice coffee table. I also wasn't as nervous as I sat down across from him.

I quickly started the interview.

"Pat, I'd like to ask you about your experience and strategies regarding people with fetal alcohol spectrum disorders or intellectual disabilities. What is your protocol in terms of doing a suicide intervention in these types of situations?"

"I would say, on the whole, that the intervention isn't different," he said. "It's just where you put the emphasis in your approach. Those two populations share two main attributes. One, they're fairly concrete in their thinking process. Two, their level of impulsivity is very high. When you're talking about impulsivity, it's a double-edged sword. Not only do these people often move to thoughts of suicide quickly, but they also move away from them quickly, or at least they can.

"What I would say is different in terms of the assessment is that I would use fairly concrete language. The first thing I would do is definitely just listen to their emotional perspective on what's happening, which is usually said in concrete language. Then I reflect that language back to them, breaking it down in terms of a safety plan. Let's say I was writing it out for them. Maybe I'd give them a three-step option to help them self-soothe. They're a fairly distractible population and I've found, in assessment, that I can completely distract them from the topic of suicide once I've listened to what they have to say. I distract them by talking about things they enjoy. Distracting them with humor is another really simple way to take the focus off the suicidal thought. Not that you don't address it at all, but you just don't spend as much time there as you would with people without an intellectual disability. Intervention-wise, I still think all the same factors probably play into it, in terms of whether we use crisis units or relaxation. Those kinds of things still work the same. It's just a matter of simplifying it."

"So when someone like you finds out that a person has a fetal alcohol spectrum disorder or intellectual disability, what I'm understanding is that you won't even ask whether they're suicidal," I said.

"No, I wouldn't say that's true," he clarified. "I don't think that diagnosis determines whether you ask or don't ask. When somebody has chronic self-harm, chronic presentations to the ER where they're always presenting with self-harm or a suicidal gesture or threats of suicide, sometimes it's not relevant to ask that question specifically because it will always be met with a positive response. If that's the case, what do you do? If they're saying, 'Yes, I'm suicidal. Yes, I have a plan. Yes, this is what I'm going to do,' then you have to respond to that. Sometimes it's more therapeutic not to focus on that and instead dwell on issues like their emotions and mood dysregulation. All those things may lead them to feel suicidal. But you're not focusing on the suicidal piece, you're focusing on the things that lead up to that. So it's just a different focal area when somebody has chronic self-harm."

I nodded, better understanding the complexities involved. My mind then turned to another group of people: the Indigenous population.

"We know from reports in the media that Indigenous people in Canada are at higher risk for suicide, especially on the reserves," I said. "What would you consider an effective style of intervention when working with these different cultural groups, especially up north?"

Pat's face showed a mix of compassion and understanding. "Well, my experience has basically shown me that there's already a barrier as soon as I enter the room. It's a racial barrier, not only because I'm Caucasian, but because I'm approaching them in a position of authority. So I already have two strikes against me. So I try not to use medical lingo, or mental health lingo. I try to pretend as though it's just a conversation I'd have with somebody in a coffee shop. I make it very relaxed and casual. I tend not to talk a lot, because as a rule they don't tend to talk a lot either. In those situations, I think less is more. I allow them silence, which they seem fairly comfortable with, instead of filling the air with lots of questions.

"With the Indigenous population, I tend to focus more on their history and what they've seen and experienced in terms of suicide. That's often a huge factor in where they're at. There are generally patterns in play, whether they've seen a suicide or there've been recent suicides on the reserve or wherever they live. There could be a familial pattern of suicide. So I pay close attention to that, which often seems to be a driving factor. I really pay attention to the psycho-social stress they're under.

"I once had an experience that taught me a lot. I went to a reserve near Swan Lake to do a presentation on suicide prevention. When I walked in, I was the only Caucasian there in a group of about twenty board members. I gave my presentation and it was all quiet at the end. I asked whether there were any questions. One woman asked, 'Why are you here anyway?' That really made me step back and wonder, 'Yeah, like, why *am* I here?' Right? I had given this clinical presentation, but how did that pertain to the everyday horror they were living? It just made me step back and change my approach. I need to be much more real in those scenarios instead of clinical. Being clinical just doesn't work."

Listening intently, I understood what he was saying about the importance of building trust and breaking down barriers.

"So probably it would be more effective to go in there and hear what they're seeing as problems and what they want?" I inquired.

Pat nodded. "Be a facilitator instead of coming in to teach them."

The conversation then shifted to the impact of isolation on young people and its connection to suicide.

"How much does isolation play into the role of suicide for young people?" I asked. "For example, in terms of not having enough resources out there or a lot of things for people to do in the community?"

"It is a factor. Boredom is always a factor, right? Because if you don't have meaning in your life or a sense of worth and purpose, then you'll feel a huge sense of hopelessness as soon as you're bored and undistracted. I would use that word, hopelessness, over anything else. It's a really vicious cycle. I've sat across from a lot of Indigenous teens who want to get off the reserve so badly. They want to come to the big city and make a better life for themselves, to get educated and break away. But they face so much pressure. They're worried they will be rejected or shunned from their community, and that's often the reality for them. They essentially end up having to choose between a better life or community acceptance.

"But often they get neither. I've been with people who've chosen the better life. They've tried to better themselves and tried to reintegrate back into the community to contribute in some way. And they get rejected because people think, 'Oh, you're too good for us now. You had to go somewhere else.' It's not dissimilar to the Hutterites, who are often shunned for wanting to break away and try to do something else with their lives. It's a real catch-22."

I felt deeply moved by the struggles faced by these young individuals he was describing.

"I suppose it's hard to reintegrate yourself back into the community once you're out," I remarked.

"You're not really accepted because you've tried to prove yourself."

As the conversation continued, I couldn't help but ponder a larger question. "I want to take this topic to a global scale. Why is suicide such a big problem in our world?"

Pat took a moment to gather his thoughts. "Well, that's a really huge question. I don't have an answer for it. But I do see some patterns in society that contribute to it. Regardless of the group, it seems that people aren't as resilient as they used to be—at least in North America. People are used to instant gratification. They're used to having their needs met quickly. When life throws them a curveball or their needs aren't met, they don't seem to have the capacity to self-soothe. They haven't developed the coping skills to get through tough times. They want a quick fix—and suicide is a pretty quick fix when life looks bad. More and more, we have this mindset as a society—instant gratification, constant stimulation, and avoiding pain. We're doing these things more and more. Over the years, the stigma has decreased in terms of suicide. Although that's a good thing overall, I think for some people there's more acceptance of it. That's a double-edged sword."

I was struck by the deep implications of societal shifts and their impact on people's mental health. However, my curiosity was leading me to dig deeper.

"Our seniors are often ignored, and they have alarming rates of suicide too," I said. "They represent eighteen to twenty percent of our population, and it's been estimated that about thirty-five percent of seniors, those sixty-five and older, will consider or attempt or die by suicide. Why do you feel this group is so often ignored and not talked about more?"

"I wonder if this has to do with ageism," Pat replied. "If a child dies tragically, it's all over the media. It just seems so wrong, and such a big loss, to die prematurely. When it's a senior, though, people may think, 'They were close to death. They lived a good life.' Maybe they were isolated and didn't have a lot of connection. Our way of gauging that loss is just different than with a child or contributing adult or somebody with a family.

"It doesn't surprise me that the suicide rate is that high. It stems from a sense of isolation and the loss of purpose. Yeah, there can be a disconnectedness from family and the loss of their role in life. Often they're living close to poverty too, and they're in chronic pain. All those factors increase their risk of suicide. Their perspective would probably be, 'Yeah, I've lived my life. I've done what I've wanted to do. My family doesn't need me anymore.' So it might seem more acceptable for them to consider that option.

"I recently saw a gentleman who was over seventy-five years old. He'd recently retired from a career he'd done all his life. He told me that his family had moved on with their lives and really didn't need him much. They came around once in a while, he felt, out of obligation. Many of his friends had died as well, so he felt isolated. He had loved what he did for a living, but he wasn't able to do it anymore. So he had no purpose. He hadn't developed any hobbies, and he was financially struggling. I sat across from him and thought, 'Yeah, I get it! Look at all these losses you have.' He wasn't able to identify things in his life that gave him joy. I did the full suicide assessment and he denied that he was suicidal. He essentially said, 'No, that's not something I would think about.' Very shortly after that, he took his life. It was shocking to some degree, because he hadn't talked about it. But it also wasn't shocking when I thought about what his life looked like at that point. I think he was fairly hopeless. Most seniors grew up thinking that suicide was unacceptable. I'm not saying it's acceptable now, but it's certainly talked about more."

Hearing this story, I felt a deep concern for seniors who might be silently suffering. I decided to inquire about the impact of losing independence and its relation to suicide among the elderly.

"How much does losing independence affect older people, and the realization that they need more help?" I asked. "You talked about worth and dignity, so I wonder if those are contributing factors."

"Yeah, for sure. The word I probably hear the most is 'burden.' People feel, at that age and in that situation, that they're a burden for their families. Not being around anymore is the only way they can think of to ease that burden, right? People aren't stupid. They see what's coming. They see their loss of independence. They see a different life, possibly in a personal care home. They see the loss of dignity, and maybe pain and sickness. The desire to avoid that is probably fairly strong, whether people talk about it or not."

I couldn't help but feel empathetic for the sadness faced by these vulnerable seniors.

"Is there any typical method they would seek out to take their lives, whether it's something as extreme as a gun or—"

"This gentleman I talked about had a gun," he said. "When you're talking about males in a rural area, gun ownership isn't uncommon. But they tend to use less violent methods. Generally, I would say it's an overdose."

"Because they often have a lot of pills and medications accessible to them?"

"Or they might stop taking certain medications. The opposite effect. Whether it's their diabetic medication or their heart medication, it's a more passive method."

I couldn't shake off the sorrow I felt. "You talked about non-violent, more subtle methods. What comes to my mind is dying by carbon monoxide poisoning."

"That's one. Men more than women," Pat acknowledged. "Suicide just seems like more of an option now, especially with it appearing in the media more often. And especially with the passing of the bill for physician-assisted suicide."

"Do you feel there's a push?" I asked. "Are there more and more doctors agreeing with medical assistance in dying? Or are doctors feeling like they're going against their own Hippocratic oath, failing to do everything possible to sustain human life?"

"I don't know if I could really comment on that well. Or at least, not accurately. Just within the circle of psychiatry, that's a very different issue. In most cases, mental illness isn't seen as a chronic, debilitating, incurable disease, so it wouldn't be relevant for physician-assisted suicide. But there are situations where it would be. It's not so much that it would be difficult to obtain this from a physician, but that only a very small population of people would be in favor of going through that process."

That answer gave me pause.

"So why does it seem like there's such a big push with our current federal government?" I asked. "MAiD was introduced only for adults who are competent with terminal illnesses. Now we seem to be adding other groups of people who are eligible. For example, people with disabilities and our senior populations. We're also seeing people with mental health issues consider it. Some countries have gone as far as to introduce medical assistance in dying to children without parental consent. For example, in Belgium."

"I don't know the answer to that," Pat said. "As soon as you open a conversation about that, every group is going to come out of the woodwork and say, 'Well, we should be eligible.' It just opens the conversation up. I don't think the legislation will honestly incorporate all those groups. And even if it does, I think the public doesn't have a complete understanding of what this will look like. I think it will be very difficult to end up obtaining physician-assisted suicide. The number of hoops people have to jump through, the number of assessments that have to happen... it's not going to be a free-for-all."

In response, I chose to bring up the political aspect of medical assistance in dying. I wanted to draw attention to the fact that MAiD would cause professionals and patients alike to confront their moral boundaries.

"So the current government here in Manitoba has passed a bill mandating that doctors who aren't in agreement don't have to participate in medical assistance in dying," I said. "It seems like the federal government in Ottawa has moved forward believing they will get support from the medical field, but they seem to lack that support here in Manitoba. What do you think causes this contradiction?"

"When MAiD gets closer, people will start drawing clearer lines. They won't make it until they're forced into that position. As the law gets closer, people will stand their ground on certain matters. As a physician, if you opt not to do this, you still have to provide a referral to someone who will. That's your obligation to the patient. At our health centre, given that we're a faith-based organization, the majority of our physicians are not in favor of MAiD for a variety of reasons. Some are in favor. My perspective is that most here will not want to take an active role in this."

At that time, I expressed gratitude for Pat taking the time to meet me and acknowledged the stress that his work entails, including the emotional toll of listening to and supporting those facing life-altering decisions.

Afterward I reflected on the interview, such as Pat's concerns for the wellbeing of Indigenous communities, our senior population, and vulnerable people with disabilities, particularly in the context of end-of-life decisions. My own personal experiences added emotional weight, since my in-laws were living with me and Trudy at the time. And as for medical assistance in dying, the contradictions and ethical dilemmas raised concerns for myself, but also for healthcare professionals and those who are part of vulnerable populations.

CHAPTER TWO

Dark Soul of the Night

WHEN CONSIDERING THE people affected by suicide, some groups are often overlooked, like medical professionals. I was reminded of this by my friend, Pat Gerbrandt, who shared the heartbreaking story of a doctor in Steinbach, Manitoba who took his life a few years ago. This prompted me to reach out to Barb Hamm, the doctor's wife, to discuss her husband's experience.

Our conversation took place on a sunny day at her country home. As I shook Barb's hand, I could sense the pain she carried. She opened up about her husband, Dr. Richard Hamm, a family physician who tragically died by hanging in their garage just before a family trip.

Unfortunately, I later discovered that I had lost the entire recording, which left me devastated. I hesitated to ask for another interview, so I set the story aside for almost four years. However, I felt compelled to give it another try and sent Barb interview questions via email. She kindly replied, sharing her insights and experiences related to suicide.

Barb revealed that her husband had once admitted to contemplating self-harm during his struggle with depression. Still, at the time of his suicide he hadn't disclosed anything beforehand, despite his emotional distress. Additionally, Barb shared the heart-wrenching experience of watching her daughter battle an eating disorder, which led to a suicide attempt. Their story opened the doors for others to share their journeys through suicidal ideation.

She currently works as a receptionist for her church and strives to be a supportive presence to those who struggle, acknowledging their pain to let them know they aren't alone. She highlights the importance of open discussions about mental health and the need for us to walk alongside one another, especially during times of isolation and loneliness.

When asked about the effectiveness of her profession in responding to people who are suicidal or bereaved by suicide loss, Barb believes that the life and hope offered through Jesus Christ is a powerful response to the heart cry of people from all walks of life. She acknowledges that there is always room for improvement in supporting one another in this world.

Reflecting on society's response to suicide, Barb feels we are doing the best we can with the therapies and treatments available, but she emphasizes the importance of recognizing the effective alternatives that can complement traditional medical practices.

In terms of improving our response to suicide, Barb emphasizes the better integration of therapies and the realization that each of us can play a role in speaking words of life and healing into each other's lives.

She acknowledges the gravity of the suicide crisis, which is only increasing in our world amidst great uncertainty. Having lost her husband to suicide, Barb still grapples with numbness and wonders whether she could have done more. However, she finds strength in her faith walk and holding onto the truth that each individual is precious and loved.

Her story serves as a poignant reminder that none of us are immune from experiencing dark nights of the soul—times when we forget the truth of our inherent worth and the love of our Creator. She advocates for kindness and dispelling any prejudice that leads us to assume that those who appear to have it all together are always okay.

Barb's email concluded by expressing her curiosity about respectful ways to address the need for mental health care when it may not be immediately apparent. Her hope is that we can find ways to provide support and care in the face of helplessness.

This interview has solidified my belief that no one is immune to suicidal thoughts or the impact of suicide. The years of COVID-19 have only heightened my concerns over reports of medical professionals who succumb to suicide. Barb attached a family picture to the bottom of her email, reminding me of the importance of counting our blessings each day and acknowledging that no one is exempt from the effects of suicide.

CHAPTER THREE

Suicide and Mental Health

MEETING JON REYES, a Member of the Legislative Assembly (MLA) for the St. Norbert constituency and Special Envoy for Military Affairs for Manitoba's provincial government, was a nerve-wracking experience. The receptionist warned me that he was very busy and could only spare about fifteen minutes for the interview, adding to my anxiety.

As I entered his office at the Legislature in Winnipeg, I noticed a picture of a young Jon Reyes in his military uniform. Though he appeared brave, there was a deep intensity in his eyes, suggesting that he had experienced difficulty and trauma during his time as a soldier.

After exchanging handshakes, I explained that the interview would revolve around the sensitive topic of suicide, that I was gathering information for my upcoming book. Mr. Reyes mentioned that he had personal experience with suicide and that it would be a challenging discussion.

Feeling a bit overwhelmed, I reminded myself of the limited time we had and the importance of asking my questions efficiently. To establish a connection and convey transparency, I decided to share my own story first. I revealed that I was a survivor of suicide, having attempted to take my life at the age of eighteen. However, I managed to overcome those challenges and found a new path in life. Now I was teaching an ASIST workshop and providing suicide intervention training.

Despite my nerves, sharing my story felt like the right approach, as it allowed me to be genuine and empathetic. I hoped the personal connection would enable us to have a meaningful and insightful conversation.

As the interview began, Mr. Reyes responded positively to my passion for helping people at risk of suicide. My personal sharing seemed to have put him at ease.

That's when I fired off my first question: "How often do people disclose to you that they're contemplating suicide?"

"Personally, I haven't had anyone disclose that they're contemplating suicide," he replied. "I know people who have been depressed and I think it's very important to listen and be around them to keep in touch and follow up. But in terms of people disclosing whether they're contemplating suicide, I haven't had that experience fortunately."

"What would be your protocol when someone discloses? How would you respond to a suicidal person?"

He replied graciously. "I guess for me it would be about listening, obviously. Listening respectfully. And then reassuring them that I'm here to listen. I'd recommend that they get help—to contact professionals, counsellors, doctors, and a community group with specialized practitioners. In Winnipeg, Klinic would be one establishment that could help out if people were depressed. So that's my knowledge, but listening is key."

"What are the biggest challenges your profession faces when it comes to suicide?"

"Well, you know what? I guess having been in politics for two years now, what I can see is the tremendous workload that'll affect your personal life and professional life. It takes time to get to know the ropes a bit better. One challenge is spending more time with my family, but sometimes I go through my ups and downs. Fortunately, I haven't ever contemplated suicide. I can tell you that personally because I'm surrounded by some really good, positive people. If I ever need help, I won't be too shy to ask for it. I think that's one of the reasons I can be there to listen to people if they need help. I'll tell them I'm there for them. I think that's key."

At that point, Mr. Reyes looked at me and asked a question of his own: "Would you agree with that?"

I paused and looked back at him, feeling confused. I had thought I was on a timeline, but now it seemed like he wanted to talk more.

"I do agree with that," I replied. "Listening is a big part of doing a good intervention. People contemplating suicide are in a headspace they call head fog, where they feel they're not being heard. They feel like their nonverbals are speaking for them loud and clear, telling people that they're in trouble. People are not able to detect these signs and one of the biggest reasons, I believe, is that we're just not trained to pick up on body language and nonverbals. That's where the ASIST training comes in. It helps you to detect people who might be in trouble. It also teaches us how to engage in the kind of critical conversation that's very uncomfortable for a lot of people. We need to stay in that difficult conversation by hearing and listening to their stories."

It was then time to refocus and go back to my questions.

"In your opinion, how effective is your profession in responding to people who are suicidal, and to people who are bereaved by suicide loss? So it's kind of a two-part question."

"I think we can do better as a society to support people through the grief process," he said. "I think we need to help lift the stigma of suicide. Recently, a friend of mine unfortunately committed suicide. He had a young family and his wife... I can't imagine. Let's just put it this way: I can't imagine. I think he had everything going for him. A beautiful wife. Beautiful kids. He'd just graduated and wanted to get his career going. And there were no signs. There were no signs! Like, no one knew, and it was a shock. A total shock. On the outside, you know, he had a beautiful family, they owned a house, the future was looking great. All of a sudden, this happens. I was shocked. So what I do now is I reach out to her from time to time and say, 'Hey, if you need anything, if you want the kids to come visit me at the lake, tell me. Let me know if you need anything.' There are also post-suicide professionals who can help people, right?"

Mr. Reyes looked very sad sharing that story. Noticing that he was deeply impacted by his friend's suicide, I waited a bit so he could regain his composure.

"You're right," I finally said, trying to maintain my own composure while shaking off the sadness lingering in the room. "I mean, there is the post-intervention that needs to happen for this family. I think that's why we have a lot of people who are suffering in silence, because people don't know there are resources out there to help them. There are people like this mother you describe, with her family grieving..."

I paused for a moment, trailing off.

"I think as a society we can always improve," Mr. Reyes said. "We can do a better job, right? Those who are contemplating suicide and those, like you said, dealing with the after-effects. We can always improve so we can prevent these situations."

I sensed now that Mr. Reyes cared deeply about the topic of suicide, for it had affected him in a profound way. The sadness was swirling and I felt myself getting more and more absorbed.

"What, in your opinion, could be done to improve how we deal with the problem of suicide?" I asked.

"I don't think talking about suicide causes people to turn to suicide. Sons, daughters, parents, and colleagues… we must reach out to them. Especially if we see changes in a person's mood and behavior. It's very important."

"How big do you think the suicide crisis is in this world?"

"You know, we go through a lot of stresses in life, and we live in a faster-paced world. Do you have children?"

I smiled and looked up with tears welling up. "Yes."

"Okay, so do you feel that you're a lot busier as a parent than your own parents were?"

"I think we're heavily tasked with more responsibilities at work than our parents were."

"I know you're supposed to be asking the questions, but…"

I hesitated. "Thank you for asking. I agree. We live in a very fast-paced world that requires us to sometimes make quick decisions on the spot. I think we're bombarded with daily work decisions that my parents' generation didn't have. I have a feeling, Mr. Reyes, that we're similar in age."

He smiled. "Yeah."

"I think my parents' job description was a lot different. I think they were focused on one to two, maybe three tasks per day at their jobs. I find myself bombarded with at least twenty-five to thirty-five tasks per day. A lot of my tasks have to do with decision-making. I think that kind of pressure really adds to our mental health, and it affects our general health as well. Stress is definitely a killer."

I felt like Mr. Reyes and I were starting to connect and relate to each other.

"You know, I want to touch on the subject of mental health because I served for ten years in the military," he pointed out. "Suicides happened quite frequently, unfortunately, in the Canadian Armed Forces. I happen to have a friend who went to Afghanistan. And on the second day, there's already a repatriation ceremony. Somebody already passed away and they did a ceremony. The second day he was there. So how does that affect an individual like my friend? During his six months there, he saw stuff that you could not imagine. When he came back, we were happy to see him. His wife had a child, she got pregnant, and all of a sudden Haiti had an earthquake. I think he had a week or two with his family before he was sent to Haiti.

"I'm just speaking from the Canadian Armed Forces perspective and being a veteran. We can do a lot more. We've got to listen more. I reach out to that friend from time to time because he's in Ottawa now. Monthly I'll shoot him a text. There was one point when things went dark and I wasn't getting any response, and neither were our other friends across the country. I was asking, 'Have you heard from him?' Turned out it wasn't just me, so it's not like I did something wrong. Suicide and mental health obviously tie in together, and I think we have to continue to improve at listening. I applaud you for doing this interview, because we have to listen to people like yourself. You can communicate this message to people who are suffering. We don't want suicide to happen, obviously."

My heart sank as I tried to imagine what his friend must have gone through. I pictured his wife and children crying, barely seeing him when he returned home before he had to rush to another crisis in a different country.

But I had to continue the interview.

"From your experience with the military, can you talk a little bit about post-traumatic stress disorder, or PTSD? How does it affect people? For example, you have soldiers, like you said, trained for combat who see these horrific scenes. They may live on the battlefield for a while and then come home. All of a sudden, these feelings from the battlefield resurface and make it difficult to cope. Do you feel that military people with PTSD have a higher risk of suicide versus the average person in the workforce?"

"As a veteran myself, when I used to be in the military, we have a job that's not the average job. So my answer, my personal answer, is that, yes, they are at higher risk. Unfortunately, we had a member from one of the reserve units commit suicide in Shilo a couple of months ago. I believe it was last year. When I got the news, I learned it was a young man with a bright future ahead of him. It's always a sad day when that happens—and not just in the military, but for everybody. Obviously you wonder to yourself, 'What could I have done? What could that family have done? You know, how come we didn't see this?' I know that's off-topic, but I think it relates."

"What do you think the numbers are in terms of military people with PTSD?"

"I don't know the exact numbers. It's always been an issue, even when I joined back in 1990. But I don't have the exact figures. I could definitely get you those if you wanted. It's probably easy to look up."

"Send me an email when you get a chance," I kindly replied. "I think you've already answered this question, but we'll go back to it. How has suicide impacted you in your own life?"

"The first time I actually saw somebody commit suicide, I was going to school. Lo and behold, one of the playground instructors and I saw somebody hanging. It was early in the morning and—"

"—in public?"

"Yeah, in public. That was my first experience seeing something like that."

This really spooked me. I tried to imagine that horrible scene.

"How old were you?" I asked.

"I believe I was either fifteen or sixteen. You know, when you're a teenager you don't see those things. I mean, you *hear* of those things. You may encounter it in movies, but you never see it in real life. So that had an impact on me. I've seen people attempt to commit suicide. When I was in Halifax, I saw somebody on a bridge... and fortunately someone was able to talk that individual out of it. And there was another friend of mine who unfortunately committed suicide. That was a year and a half ago when he did this. He was in the military, and he committed suicide. So we have to do more, that's all I can say. We have to do more."

I felt compelled to help. "Do you know whether there's any training right now happening in the military with ASIST? Applied Suicide Intervention Skills Training?"

"Well, I know there's PTSD training in the military now. That's very important. And when I was in the Forces, I remember there was always somebody coming around and talking about the reality of our occupations, about how stressful it was. They'd always have a subject matter expert, I guess, if you'd want to call it that, come talk to soldiers, sailors, and airmen."

I went back to an earlier question. "And for those who don't know what PTSD is, how would you describe it?"

He carefully thought through his answer. "It's something that, I guess for me, is something that will never, ever go away. You just have to cope with it and talk it out. You just have to be there for the person who has it. You have to be their sounding board, because they've experienced something no one else has. That's why, for me, it's very important to be there for my friend even though he's in Ottawa. I'm there to listen. It's just very important to listen to people who have that condition. And it's never going to go away. It will always be there, in the person's experiences. But as an outside person, you don't see it."

I leaned in, wanting to understand. "If PTSD never goes away, is that because it constantly revisits a person and can catch them off-guard? Like, they can be having a great day and suddenly they get triggered and taken back to that place? To them, they're back in that reality, reliving a trauma? Is that what happens? I agree that intervention is so important, to check up on people. It's key to make sure they know they have support, that people care and they aren't alone. That consistent support, I think, helps people to stay around."

Mr. Reyes nodded. "They may say 'I'm fine,' but they're not. Or the pain will come back. People do improve, their condition improves, but in my opinion, from my experience of knowing people who suffer from PTSD, it never goes away. They just have to live with it. We can help them cope by being a sounding board. People feel a sense of relief when we communicate with them, right? If we keep checking up on them and stay in touch, it lets them know that we're there for them. It adds value for both people."

"Absolutely!" I said. "You've talked about how this makes you feel. But how do you deal with those feelings, knowing that your friends are in trouble? Like you said, it almost seems hopeless. And yet I think there is hope for people with PTSD. As a society, we need to become better listeners. I also think it's therapeutic for people to verbalize their intense pain and talk it out. When people feel heard, they don't feel alone anymore. So being good listeners is the key."

"Yup."

We were both starting to get it. We valued the same things about people dealing with poor mental health and suicidal thoughts.

I continued to press. "What else would you like to share about the topic of suicide?"

"I think what we're doing now—openly discussing the topic of suicide. I think you're doing a commendable job with these interviews because you get different perspectives. I mean, obviously I share a unique perspective, because of my experience with the military. But everyone is going to have a different perspective. We have to collect the thoughts and ideas of various people, take it all in, and then communicate the message in a positive way so we can prevent suicides from happening."

Hearing his feedback filled me with hope. Maybe I was on the right track with this project, seeking out people in different fields to face the topic from alternate points of view.

But I still had one more questions.

"What else would you like to know about suicide?" I asked.

"What I'd like to know is, why do people think this way? And how can we prevent people from thinking this way? Because we all go through a lot of stress in life and people deal with stress in different ways. I think the best thing to do is gather information and communicate effectively with people who suffer from poor mental health that can lead them to suicide. How can we prevent that? That's my question. What can we gather from these interviews you're doing? Can we communicate with people who are contemplating suicide?"

I could sense his desperation to understand, to help people with mental health challenges and mental illness. Sometimes we don't get the answers to difficult questions, or at least we don't get pat answers.

I took a deep breath and calmed myself. I'd been in my own tough places mentally, times when it was really hard to make sense of what was going on. In those moments, I had to take refuge in God to protect my mind from overthinking and pulling me into heavy negativity.

As we concluded the interview, I stood up, compelled to offer comfort to this compassionate soul. Thanking him for his time, I shook his hand warmly and expressed my gratitude for his work and service to our country.

As I left Mr. Reyes's office, I reflected on the powerful stories shared during our conversation. I couldn't help but feel hopeful that through open dialogue, empathy, and support, we could create a world in which suicide could be prevented, in which mental health would be more greatly valued.

My visit with Mr. Reyes left a lasting impact on me, and I knew his efforts would make a significant difference in the lives of those he touched.

CHAPTER FOUR
People Services

MY ANTICIPATION IN meeting Mr. Duane Brothers after so many years was palpable. As I entered his home, I could sense the weight of his emotions, evident in the closed curtains and tired look in his eyes.

Even as we greeted each other and I began to record our conversation, I felt unsure whether this was the right time for the interview.

"So the first thing I'll ask you is to clarify your title, Mr. Brothers."

"I'm Dr. Brothers, and I'm the superintendent of the Louis Riel School Division."

Dr. Brothers was my former geography teacher at Daniel Macintyre High School in 1986. But today he seemed distant, and I understood that he might not remember me from among the countless students he had taught over his career.

Sitting in his living room, surrounded by pictures of his children, I explained that we were discussing the topic of suicide for an upcoming book I was writing.

"How often do people disclose to you that they're contemplating suicide in your line of work?" I asked.

"Directly to me? Very rarely do I hear about it. People tend to disclose to staff members, like directors of student support services or human resources. But not directly to me."

I inquired about the protocol in such situations and Dr. Brothers explained that it was important to move very quickly.

"Our protocol involves contacting Child and Family Services if someone discloses such thoughts. It's the responsibility of anyone, be it a teacher or otherwise, to disclose this information immediately. We aim to educate our teachers to recognize challenging behaviors and the needs of our students beyond just teaching the curriculum."

"What are the biggest challenges your profession faces when it comes to suicide?"

"The intensification of stress in our society is a significant challenge. Kids feel pressured to look and dress a certain way, while adults face stress related to finances and maintaining extravagant lifestyles. Many adult relationships break down due to this pressure. High school students, in particular, experience excessive stress to achieve high marks and excel in exams to secure a spot in university. It's overwhelming. We have a successful society, but it's also a stressed-out one."

I couldn't help but wonder about the effectiveness of the education system's response to those who are either suicidal or bereaved by loss through suicide.

"We're getting better," he said. "Over the last two years, we've made changes in the Louis Riel School Division. We shifted the name of our human resources department to people services, emphasizing that our staff members aren't just resources but individuals who work with us for the betterment of our kids and community. We aim to create a better workplace and set life boundaries for our staff, knowing that this will positively impact our kids and the community. It's an ongoing effort, and we still have a long way to go."

I then sought his perspective on what could be done to improve how society deals with the problem of suicide.

He paused thoughtfully. "We need to continue improving. Changing the orientation from human resources to people services has been purposeful, but there is more to be done. We should work towards creating a more supportive environment for our staff and students, emphasizing the importance of mental health and wellbeing. Education and awareness are crucial, and we should foster open dialogue to reduce the stigma surrounding suicide. We need to do a much better job with young people and adults alike to open the door and allow them to talk about when they're not well and know that it's okay. If somebody breaks their arm, it's easy to talk about it. But we don't make it easy for people to talk about when they're not feeling well in their mind, and we have to do that. Increasingly it's got to be leaders like me, who struggle with sadness, to expose our sadness so we can find a way to help others and get them the help they need."

"How big do you think the suicide crisis is?"

"You know what? I can't speak definitively. I know that some kids commit suicide. I'm aware of a couple of staff members who have committed suicide in the last couple of years. What I can speak definitively about is the huge proportion of staff and students who deal with significant levels of mental unwellness."

I could tell that Dr. Brothers was having a tough time throughout this interview and I empathized with his struggles. This led to more questions.

"Has suicide impacted you in any way in your own lifetime?"

"Myself? I've had periods of deep depression, sadness, and loss. But I personally have never felt suicidal."

"Do you know anyone in your family, circle of friends, colleagues, or community who has attempted or died by suicide?"

"I don't."

Though he appeared to carry a weight of sorrow, he remained gracious and patient with me. I appreciated his honesty and transparency.

He went on sharing. "Well, in my job as a superintendent, we come back to the idea that staff aren't just resources. They are people. And if I'm really doing my job, I've got to increasingly create work environments where people can be healthy, physically and mentally healthy, and supported. This means we can decrease the amount of absenteeism, and people can feel better about themselves. They can have better work-life balance and be better role models for students. We have to do a much better job, and we're getting there, of teaching mindfulness to our kids. It's got to be more than just covering the curriculum. To be blunt about it, a benefit I have is that I've dealt with this, which helps me to stay open."

"What else would you like to know or share about the topic of suicide?"

"If somebody gets to a point where they feel so low that they want to commit suicide, it's a pretty nasty place to be. Because you know what? Everybody's created by God to live in purpose. I do know that some people will talk about suicide, and it's just their way of reaching out for help, right? It shouldn't be that way. Somebody shouldn't have to talk about being suicidal for them to be open to assistance. Then we have another group of people who actually do attempt real suicide, and some of them actually accomplish it, which puts a bigger emphasis on this question: how do we as a community allow people to get to such a place? I'd like to know more about it for myself, and for my staff to recognize the signs of people who are potentially suicidal. I'd like to be more knowledgeable, for me and my staff, about helping our community. And by the community, I mean our staff, our students, and our parent community, to look after themselves better. Again, I've said it a couple of times, but it's got to be about more than the curriculum. We don't just teach reading and writing and arithmetic."

As I left Dr. Brothers's home, I couldn't shake off the weight of the discussion. Although it had been emotionally draining, I recognized the importance of sharing these stories with the world.

CHAPTER FIVE
Suicide Affects Everybody

ANDREW MICKELFIELD WAS a familiar face from my past. I had heard him speak at a church my wife attended in 2002. Later, he became the principal of that church's private school and eventually he was elected as an MLA, like Jon Reyes.

Intrigued by Andrew's unique perspective, I tracked him down for an interview, eager to hear his thoughts on suicide and the experiences he had encountered throughout his diverse career.

We decided to meet at an old family restaurant in Winnipeg's St. Vital neighborhood to have coffee and talk.

"It's December 12, 2017, and I'm interviewing Andrew Mickelfield, the MLA for Rossmere. We're discussing the topic of suicide, specifically Bill 34 that passed in legislation. Andrew, could you tell us more about this bill?"

"Bill 34 is a Manitoba-specific legislation that reaffirmed conscience rights for medical professionals who are uncomfortable with participating in medically assisted death," Andrew explained.

Curious to understand its implications, I probed further. "How does this law protect a doctor? Can they object to referrals or participation in assisted suicide?"

"The Supreme Court ruled that every Canadian has the right to access medically assisted death, also known as assisted suicide or euthanasia. While doctors in Manitoba are not required to participate in the act, they must provide information to patients seeking such services. So while this bill does not entirely exempt doctors, it's a significant step forward in conscience protections."

"How often do people disclose to you that they're contemplating suicide, either in your professional field or personal life?"

"In my role as an MLA, it's not something that happens regularly. It's not part of a typical or even atypical workweek or month for me," Andrew replied thoughtfully. "On a personal level, suicide affects everyone to some extent, but thankfully it's not something I encounter often."

As we ordered coffees from the waitress, I asked another question. "In your opinion, what are the biggest challenges your profession faces when it comes to suicide?"

"Politicians, like myself, do face many challenges, but suicide isn't one that commonly arises in our line of work. However, the pain of suicide is felt heavily in some communities, especially among our Indigenous population. The suicide rates among Indigenous people are alarmingly high, and that's deeply concerning."

Despite the restaurant's lively ambiance, I found myself drawn to Andrew's insights and genuine concern for the wellbeing of the community he served.

"How do you think society is handling the issue of suicide?" I asked. "What are we doing right, and what are we doing wrong?"

Andrew paused for a moment. "You know, it's a difficult question. As long as somebody is contemplating taking their life, we're obviously not getting that part right. However, I think the topic has become something people can talk about more openly in the last five or ten years, and that's a good thing. Maybe counterintuitively, there are ways it can be talked about that are not helpful. So I think we have quite a distance to go, but it's good that people don't have to feel like they're alone on this one."

"What, in your opinion, could be done to improve how we deal with the problem of suicide?"

"Before this interview, I didn't know that you were involved in the ASIST program. As I pondered this question last night and this morning, I think that programs like ASIST have a good track record. The data behind them demonstrates that they do good work, and they have measurable results. I only mention ASIST because it's one training program I know about. I'm sure there are other good programs out there as well."

From my own work with ASIST, I knew that the workshops increase the chances of saving a life to about twenty percent. While that may not seem high, the chance of reviving someone through CPR is only about ten percent. Despite the low percentages, I emphasize the value of making every effort and offering every possible support.

"Has suicide impacted you in any way in your lifetime?" I asked, acknowledging the sensitivity of the topic.

"Oh sure. My friend's father ended his life. When I was a teenager, I worked with people who ended their lives. I also know people who've requested and accessed medically assisted death. Although someone else may squeeze the needle, I count that as a form of suicide, so it's never far away from any of us."

"Do you know anyone in your circle of friends, your colleagues, or community who has attempted or died by suicide?"

"In the early 1990s, my mother went through a very dark depression that lasted for four years. I know that suicide was frequently close to her mind during that time. I don't think she ever actually attempted, but I think she certainly walked very close to the line more than once during those dark years. I'm not dispassionate about it. I'm very aware that this isn't an academic issue. It's a very real problem. For people facing it, it's all-consuming. I hope this gives me compassion and empathy for people who are dealing with it, either personally or with a loved one."

As he spoke, Andrew's voice expressed sincerity and genuine concern.

"How have you dealt with these feelings?" I inquired, wanting to understand how he coped with the emotional weight of such experiences.

"Well, you know, I hope it makes me a more compassionate person. I don't know how to deal with them. I actually think those are good feelings to have. I think we shouldn't look away from some of the difficult things in our society, and this is one of them."

"What else would you like to share about the topic of suicide?"

"I don't know of the status of this group, but I believe it was recently identified that men over forty are vulnerable, and that was a bit of a surprise to me. I'm sure research has been done. We need to not stereotype about who struggles with these things, but we all need to take care of our own health, in every sense— spiritually, mentally, physically, and emotionally. I think our culture is full of toxic components which can drag us down the wrong path. I think we need to identify those and choose not to take them in, the same way we might be good at identifying anything that's toxic for our physical bodies. We're mental, emotional, and spiritual people as well. We need to take the same precautions in those categories."

I was curious to understand what specific areas he believed needed more attention or research.

"What would you like to know more about in terms of suicide?" I inquired.

"That's a difficult question. Anything I can learn that could help save someone's life is something I'd like to know more about," he replied earnestly. "I know we've developed pretty good protocols for being able to assess people who are having a heart attack or if they've collapsed. The ABC protocol—airways, breathing, circulation—for CPR has saved many lives. If there could be a similar protocol developed for people who are suicidal or not doing well mentally, hopefully that could become part of the public narrative, and people could learn to take care of themselves, but also care for each other as well.

"Like I say, we're not just physical beings. Although there may be chemical reasons for people thinking of suicide, we are holistic people. We need a whole community to come around us. We need to be part of a community so we can more adequately be prepared for some of these things so we don't just deal with them when they hit us or others."

This really jolted me. I thought about the future for my parents and in-laws.

"Why is it that our seniors seem so often to be ignored?" I said. "We don't seem to think that they could be at high risk for suicide."

"I don't know what the data is there, so I'm guessing a little bit," Andrew replied thoughtfully. "My constituency has a very high number of seniors per capita, one of the largest in the province. You know, I can appreciate on an intellectual level the difficulties of having a productive and social life, and then suddenly you realize your body can't do what it used to, and maybe your mind can't do what it used to. Seniors face some significant changes. Perhaps their children move away or a spouse dies. Loneliness is not to be underestimated. Anything we can do to engage our seniors is a worthwhile use of our time."

I decided to throw out a recent stat. "I recently read a report that claimed our seniors represent eighteen percent of our population, and that thirty-five percent of them will seek out or attempt suicide. One of the things that report addressed was our senior population feeling a sense of loneliness, as you mentioned. Another contributing factor they found was seniors having low self-worth or few ways to contribute to society anymore. But some seniors engage in volunteer work. I wonder if that's a healthier approach than us just looking in on them from time to time to let them know they're still valued and appreciated."

"You know, the notion of retirement is fairly recent, when you look at human history," Andrew said. "A hundred years ago, people would work into their seventies or older. There may have been some changes over time, but they certainly didn't stop at sixty-five and just take on a new lifestyle. There are studies that demonstrate greater fulfillment in seniors who have a purpose and reason to contribute. And there are some wonderful community groups. One example is the Good Neighbours Active Living Centre in Winnipeg. Literally, they engage seniors in a variety of activities all day, every day. They do excellent work, and there are many groups like that. Churches also provide a terrific haven for seniors, and I think we should be looking more and more at how we can engage them. Schools have a lot to offer in this regard. Seniors love children, and children quite often love seniors, so I think there are some win-win scenarios we can consider as a society as we grapple with aging boomers and the implications of that for mental health and social engagement."

I nodded as I began to bring the interview to its conclusion.

"The big overarching question everybody wants to know, and I'm just seeking your opinion, is this: why do you think suicide is such a big problem in our world today?"

"Our culture has become extremely materialistic. We've attempted to find value in things. Technology has given us a lot of wonderful things, but it also leaves us empty at a very deep internal level. We have much to learn from other cultures, cultures that are more social and maybe not always as technologically advanced. But I think that we have lost something with all of our so-called progress. Maybe in other ways, we have actually stepped backward. I think we need to find balance and reconnect as communities, as individuals. We can enjoy the benefits of technology without letting it take over. There is a great hollow chasm inside us, and it can be a very dark space when it's not filled with love and community. These are things no computer or cellphone can give us."

In his voice, I detected his profound realization of the importance of genuine human connection and support. In fact, I felt relieved to hear of his caring and empathetic approach to seniors, a group often neglected and overlooked in terms of suicide prevention.

With a smile and a handshake, I concluded the meeting, expressing gratitude for Andrew's time and the meaningful work he'd done for his constituency.

My conversation with Andrew had brought forth important insights into the impact of human connection and community support in combating the darkness we sometimes face. His compassionate stance on mental health and dedication to engaging and helping seniors had left a positive impression on me, reinforcing the importance of empathy and care in addressing suicide prevention.

CHAPTER SIX

Willing to Step Alongside and Get Dirty

I'VE ALWAYS BELIEVED that to truly understand the heart of a community, province, or country, one should talk to a farmer, especially one who has been in the field a long time. These seasoned individuals are often untainted by modern media or the latest trends. They tend to live in a simple reality far removed from big tech influence and thus offer a unique perspective.

Ron Plett, a friend from my community, recommended that I interview a man named Harry Siemens. Over a cup of coffee with Ron at my home, I expressed my curiosity about the impact of suicide on our dairy farming and livestock communities. It seemed like a subject Harry might be hesitant to discuss.

Nonetheless, a few days later Ron provided me with Harry's phone number. He also informed me that Harry's wife had recently passed away. Considering the circumstances, I decided to postpone the interview and give Harry time to grieve.

However, I eventually contacted Harry and arranged to meet him at a coffee shop in Morris, Manitoba. I walked in and easily identified Harry from his description. I began by offering my condolences and suggested that we could reschedule the interview, but Harry kindly insisted that it was all right to proceed.

"I'm an advocate for farmers and have been for forty-seven years," Harry began. "I'm a farm journalist, broadcaster, and run my own website, Siemens Says."

He told me about a young fellow from Grunthal who had reached out to him two weeks earlier. They had gotten into an altercation on social media, but the man had since learned that Harry was a believer.

"He says, 'Mr. Siemens, why don't you pray for God to end everything for me?' After our disagreement, I continued to have a relationship with him. Originally he wanted to beat me up, but then he suddenly said, 'I really want to meet you and let you know that I'm not the kind of guy you think I am.' He wants to meet face to face. My latest response to him is the same as I would give anyone: 'Why are you where you are today?' Invariably I share what Jesus has done in my life and I try to get together with that person if possible. I'm not afraid to confront or be there for him."

In his profession as a journalist, Harry said that he heard many sad stories of people who thought they had secure jobs only for everything to come crashing down.

"People may get used to the accolades they've had in their public life, and suddenly it comes to an end," he said. "They don't have anything to fall back on and they may very easily be prone to take their lives. But the profession I serve, farmers, is small, maybe 1.5 percent of the population. They produce the food for the rest of the world. Not only that, but it's a pretty prestigious job. You're driving shiny new equipment, trying to rent more land, trying to do things bigger and better, etcetera."

He explained that a farmer often invests about $300 per acre before they get any return from a crop, though. During the growing season, they have no idea whether they'll get a return at all.

"All of a sudden, you come to the end of the year and you see the crop is about half of what it was going to be and you see that you're going to lose money. If you're not set up to lose money, things can be really bad. Amongst farmers, I understand the suicide rate is significantly higher than in other professions, especially in the United States. It's for exactly this reason. It's a risk some guys just can't take."

First, I was shocked to hear that any young man would want to beat up a senior citizen. Second, before this meeting I'd had no idea of the costs involved in running a farm. I agreed that it must put a huge financial strain on farmers and their families.

"How effective is your profession at dealing with suicide?" I asked.

"That's an interesting question. Someone in our church committed suicide, yet he professed to be a believer. He wrote out his testimony for me, so I was left to wonder, 'Now what do I tell the congregation?' There were a lot of people there when I shared his testimony. I said, 'I'm glad I'm not the judge, because Jesus is the ultimate judge, as to where that person will spend eternity and about what kind of decision that person made on this side.' It's interesting. I was concerned about not wanting to glorify suicide in any way, shape, or form. I think we have to be really careful. Whether I'm acting as a journalist, lay minister, or just a friend, we can't make suicide appear as a viable solution to one's problems. In my case, I walk alongside them. It's not always possible, you know. It's a real challenge, as you know far better than I. But I'm willing to work to see if I can help them or bring help."

I was starting to develop a deep appreciation for Harry. As a baby boomer, he was part of a more resilient generation than my own. I also appreciated his rugged honesty. Though those who speak their minds are often considered highly opinionated, or even arrogant, I didn't feel that was the case with Harry at all.

"How effective is society at dealing with suicide?"

"Well, I recently saw a headline that asked why we mourned the suicide of Robin Williams and celebrated the suicide of Kate Spade, a film actress and fashion designer. Isn't that interesting? I didn't read the article, although I wish I would have. At the same time, the headline itself shows that we have a real problem. One side mourns and another side celebrates suicide as a way of coming to the end of the road and hopefully solving the problem. But we know it didn't solve anything. We need people like yourself who are willing to step alongside and get dirty with people in trouble. Those people who are left behind should be given the opportunity to respond properly, and to do it in a proper setting. That's what I think needs to happen. And my wife held a position where she dealt with this as well. She was blown away by how many people were actually tempted to commit suicide because of their stressful jobs."

"What if I told you that the World Health Organization has declared suicide a world crisis? That every forty seconds a person dies by suicide?" I asked.

"Yeah. It's a real epidemic, I would say."

"Do you know anyone in your family who has attempted or died by suicide?"

"I know a number of people. I don't think I can talk about a family member, but at the same time businesspeople and so forth have actually committed suicide, and young teens. That's sad. But you have to be careful not to say, 'Oh well, that's the way it is.' That's a common response—to just move on, right? That's the caution I would give: that we don't just take the problem for granted."

"What are we doing right, and what are we doing wrong?"

"We've basically said everything that comes to my mind," Harry said. "But we need to be careful to recognize people who are actually in trouble and have the potential to commit suicide. And secondly, we need to be careful not to glorify it and make it seem like a viable option to solve their problems. That's how the world sees it, even though many won't admit it.

"I'm a journalist who likes numbers and statistics, but I'm never one to dwell on the statistics. I would much rather see the bigger picture. You know, I'm one person. When I sit down and talk to somebody, if I ask them how they're doing, I need to actually be prepared to stay and listen. We have to hear what they say. We need to make sure we're prepared to stand in the gap, so to speak, for people."

At that point, the recorder on my phone stopped, but I knew that I had gotten everything I needed. I appreciated that Harry spoke things like he saw them. He was an old country boy who perceived many issues in the farming community most of us wouldn't understand. I was pleased to have met him.

My main takeaway was what he had said about being careful not to glorify suicide as a genuine solution. I totally agreed with that. I recognized that I was just a small part of the solution, but I had a goal to create awareness and examine our attitudes about suicide. And I fully intended to conduct more interviews and hear more stories.

CHAPTER SEVEN
use the opposite weapon

IN THE WINTER of 2019, I met a concerned man who came up to me at my booth at Mission Fest, held at Church of the Rock in Winnipeg. I was there with Demetre, my cousin and co-facilitator, bringing awareness about suicide and promoting my book, *Following the Fire*. The man told me that I needed to talk to a pastor who had lost his son to suicide. I wrote down the pastor's name, Russ Toews, and later got his phone number.

Russ and I met that summer at an old church in the Westwood neighborhood of Winnipeg. I parked my car on the quiet residential street and walked towards the church.

"You don't look anything like the photo on your book cover," Russ said as he came through the door to meet me outside.

I was perplexed. Well, I wasn't currently wearing a suit like in the photo, but I didn't think I looked all that different.

We walked inside and headed to his office. I sat across from him and immediately began recording on my phone.

As the interview started, I looked up at this man who had the weight of the world on his shoulders. I could tell that he hadn't had an easy life. He was a seasoned pastor, after all.

"How often do people disclose to you that they're contemplating suicide?" I asked.

Russ reclined in his chair. "Not just myself, but including the staff here? I'd say about once a month... and it's mainly young people. But not exclusively."

Stunned, I raised my eyebrows. That was a much higher number than I would have expected.

"What is your protocol when someone discloses? How do you respond to a suicidal person?"

He gave this question some careful thought. "Each case is different, so there have been times when I've phoned a family doctor and made an appointment. The person leaves my office and goes straight to the doctor. In Winnipeg, there's a youth van that comes when called. The crisis unit at Health Sciences Centre. I've phoned them and they've come and got the kid just about immediately. That way, I can leave them with a crisis worker. I also call the parents and say, 'Come home right away. I'm calling the crisis unit. Don't leave your kid at home alone.' And the van comes within a half-hour.

"Often I'll ask, 'How are you going to do it?' And if they have a plan—for example, 'I think I'll shoot myself'—then my next question is, 'Do you have a gun and a bullet?' If they say no, then I know we have a bit of time. But they might instead say, 'I'm going to take a bunch of Tylenol-3s.' So I ask, 'Do you have a bottle?' If they reply, 'Yeah,' then I know they can leave the office and do it right away. So it depends on how urgent the situation is.

"I also have people sign a contract with me. I don't know how effective those contracts are, but they say, 'Before I harm myself, I'll call you.' My son had one of those and I found it after he died."

Russ paused his story, taking a moment to deal with the emotion.

"He had a counsellor and a best friend, and he didn't call either one of them," he continued after a few moments. "So the contracts don't always work. But I've had people return and say, 'I'm going to do it now,' and I've been able to talk them down. I'm probably leaving stuff out here, but that's what comes to mind right away. I always take it seriously. Sometimes first attempts or just contemplating suicide can be part of a person's learning curve to overcome their own fear. So yeah, always take it seriously."

I could tell that Russ had been deeply impacted by his son's death. How could any parent be otherwise? I started to feel a bit of what I must have put my own parents through when I attempted suicide back in 1988.

I knew now that this was going to be one of the toughest interviews so far. I hadn't prepared myself on how to handle my reaction if Russ disclosed how his son had died. I was walking into a realm of utter darkness, one that only a few have entered. I felt afraid of what I might find out.

"What are the biggest challenges your profession faces when it comes to suicide?"

"I think one of the biggest challenges is how to write about this or talk about it in a public setting. Because you're kind of damned if you do and damned if you don't. If you make it too pastoral, too caring, then someone who's contemplating may read it, listen, and think, 'Okay, suicide isn't too big of a deal.' The comfort and the hope might encourage people to follow through. But if you're aiming only at prevention, then people who've had somebody die would probably feel that you're being very uncaring and distant. Our denomination has a pamphlet on the subject and I read it after our son died. I thought, 'This is useless. It's not compassionate at all!' And then I realized, 'Well, if it was being read by somebody who's contemplating suicide and you made it really compassionate, it might encourage them actually to follow through.' So I think that's a big challenge. It's a catch-22. It's very controversial and requires a lot of sensitivity.

"For myself, I needed to theologically work through this question: is suicide a ticket to hell? I did a study on this, trying to discover where this theology came from. Now I believe that suicide is not a ticket to hell. Just as we don't earn our salvation, we don't lose it through sin.

"At the first funeral I performed as a pastor, I spoke about this. There were two very stark reactions. This one guy came forward, and I could see he was crying. He said, 'This is the first time in twenty-five years that I've heard there's hope for my uncle.' Now compare that to another reaction. Someone else came to me and said, 'I have a fellow in my church named Henry who has struggled with suicidal tendencies. If Henry dies by suicide, it's your fault because you've taken away his last reason not to die by suicide.' So two very different reactions. How do you address both sides of it in a public setting?"

I thought this was a very tough place to be.

"Is Henry still around?" I asked.

"That's more than thirty years ago now and, yes, Henry's still around."

"In your opinion, how effective is your profession at responding to people who are suicidal? Or those who are bereaved by suicide loss?"

"I think we're a lot better than we were thirty years ago," Russ said. "That whole idea that suicide is a ticket to hell is still prevalent among some of the older people and some of the more fundamentalist congregations. But generally, I don't think people automatically go there anymore and it's a great help to those who are bereaved. If you're dealing with the aftermath of your loved one's suicide, it's difficult to bear hearing that they're going to hell because of that. You know the old idea where those who commit suicide are buried outside the cemetery, not facing east but facing west? The church used to do that."

"How effective is the church at responding to people?"

"I'm not a counselling type of pastor, but our youth guy is. I think he's really good. He's taken suicide prevention training. The kids will talk to him about lots of very deep subjects. I think he's pretty effective. For myself, I know some of the things I'm supposed to do. But I've never had anybody threaten and then actually follow through. I've had lots of people threaten, though. It's hard to gauge how serious they were."

"So, in your opinion, how effective do you feel society is at dealing with suicide?" I probed. "What are we doing right and what are we doing wrong?"

"Well, if you just look at the numbers, our society isn't really effective. I think what we're trying to do right is make it a more common topic of discussion. It used to be such a shameful topic that we didn't talk about it at all. Now lots of people are trying to bring awareness. Out in Niverville, for example, there's the Imagine Run that's all about raising awareness about suicide. So we're doing some things right. More professional pastors and teachers getting suicide prevention training is very helpful, but again, you can only help if people are letting you know what's going on in their minds, right? If somebody is bound and determined, there isn't much you can do to stop it."

"So what could be done to improve how we deal with the problem of suicide?"

"I don't know what the answer is. But when you know that somebody is suicidal, our laws are such that you can't really lock them up, and I wouldn't want us to. At times, though, there's nothing you can do until a suicidal person makes the attempt. A friend of mine had their son institutionalized, but his son knew the game and made it seem as though he was getting healthier. He gradually earned more and more freedom, and then one day he suddenly bolted. He saw an unlocked bike outside the facility and tore off to the town water tower. He climbed up over the fence and up the tower and jumped before anyone could even respond to the fact that he had run away."

I could relate to how easy it can be to escape a hospital when you're a young man and there's hardly any monitoring. It's a subject I've written about more in my previous book, *Following the Fire*.

"How big do you think the suicide crisis is?" I asked.

"I think it's big— and there are certain pockets where it's bigger. I lived in Morden for a bunch of years. Just west of Morden, in the Darlingford-Manitou area, which is very rural, there is lots of suicide."

"Amongst farmers?" I replied with sadness. My thoughts turned to my interview with Harry Siemens, who had talked about farmers who decide to take their own lives.

"Yeah, farm people. The United Church pastor in that area was a friend of mine and he ran a Bible study. There were about ten people in the group, and after her third or fourth meeting she realized that every one of those people had a close family member who had committed suicide. That's how prevalent it was. This was back in the late 80s or early 90s."

"What do you think was the contributor out there?"

"Farm debt, I believe. You'd hear stories of a farmer getting the combine stuck and using a tractor to pull it out… and instead of pulling it out, he accidentally pulled it apart. He was already so much in debt and now his combine was destroyed. So he just went to his grain truck, put the box up, stuck his head in, and lowered the box."

I squirmed. "Ow…"

Pastor Russ could see that I was deeply saddened to hear this. "There were lots of farm deaths in those early years, and lots of drought in that part of Manitoba. Farmers were having a hard, hard time."

I managed to pull myself together. "Has suicide impacted you in any way in your own life?"

"I hadn't really thought about it very much until our son died by suicide on October 6, 2008."

"I'm so sorry to hear that. How old was he?"

"He was twenty and was going to turn twenty-one at Christmastime. It had to do with a girlfriend he had broken up with. He had talked to me about his struggles, but I never knew he was suicidal. He was a comedian. He had done a set at the comedy club in Winnipeg that summer, and it had gone well. He was well-liked at school. He was a student at Providence College in Otterburne."

My eyes welled up and I found myself struggling to get my next question out. "What was his name?"

"Brad," Russ replied with a tremble in his voice.

I softly repeated it. "Brad."

"Yeah, Brad. He was the kind of kid who was friendly to everybody but didn't have a lot of friends himself. He didn't really have that close connection with people. Looking back on it, all his life he was kind of an all-or-nothing person. He didn't want us to plan birthday parties for him, because he thought nobody would want to come. The reality is there were lots of people who wanted to come, but from his perspective he couldn't see it.

"He had a negative view of life. We'd be at some kind of function having a normal conversation with someone, and he'd come home later and say, 'That person was mad at me.' And I'd say, 'What? That person wasn't mad at you!' But that's just how he viewed things. Life became very onerous. His conclusion was that if this girl had broken up with him, and he would always be attracted to that kind of girl, then every girl he liked would always reject him. That was his conclusion."

He went on then to describe some of the details leading up to the tragedy.

"He headed down along the train tracks at 12:30 in the morning. He'd met with his girlfriend, and they'd concluded at about 10:30. He then did a couple hours of homework. Once he was on the tracks, he started walking. The train engineer saw him at roughly two o'clock, but he was hit by the train. Then he was transported by ambulance to St. Boniface Hospital, where he was pronounced dead at four o'clock. The police were at our door at ten minutes to six. That was frustrating, because all they would tell us was that he'd been hit by a train and that he was dead. They wouldn't tell us that it was suicide. We had to wait. We phoned the RCMP in St. Pierre-Jolys, but they didn't open until nine o'clock, so we waited three hours and phoned at nine."

"Where did this suicide happen?"

"About a mile south of Providence in Otterburne. There's a Canadian Pacific rail line that comes up there from the United States," he clarified. "The St. Pierre-Jolys police wouldn't talk to us on the phone, though, because they couldn't confirm who we were. We got them to agree to a plan. They would hang up, find our number in the phone book, and then call us. When they called us, they were able to tell us that it had been a suicide and there had been a note in his pocket, written on an 8.5-by-11 piece of paper. But he'd been dragged for a mile and it was raining, so there was a three-inch hole in the center of the note. The note basically said he was sorry for being such a burden, that he'd been a lousy person. The apology revealed his warped thinking because he wasn't a lousy person. He was well-liked. He wasn't a burden."

I had to take a long pause after hearing this story. I looked down towards my feet, unable to look Russ in the eye. That's how I'd felt back in 1988 when I tried to take my own life. I could relate to Brad's comments and perception of himself.

"I guess you already answered my next question," I continued slowly, my voice trembling, my heart weeping. "I was going to ask about how suicide has impacted you and your family…"

I struggled to look at my notes. My hands shook and my voice trembled. I was so impacted and I didn't know whether I could continue.

Somehow I found the strength.

"Our son is just one I know," Russ said. "The guy who was actually responsible for me becoming a pastor, the youth leader at our church, also died by suicide. He'd been institutionalized. But again, he knew how to play the game. He got a day pass to come home on a Saturday. It went so well that the staff agreed for him to stay home on Sunday. That day, he and his wife decided to have a little nap. She lay down. He lay down. A half-hour later, she woke up and he wasn't there. She started looking for him and found him hanging in the garage."

I tried to imagine how horrifying it would be to see something like that.

"Where was this?" I asked. "In Morden?"

"No. We grew up in B.C., so this was in Abbotsford." He took a moment to refocus. "Then there's the woman I told you about before, the one whose funeral I did early in my time in Morden. I was a young pastor then, at Westside Community Church, except in those days it was called the Morden Mennonite Brethren Church. She died by carbon monoxide poisoning. She left the car running in the garage and piped it into the window. At the time, I was thirty-two years old and new at the church.

"Remember what I told you about the two strong reactions to the message I spoke that day? One guy said he finally had hope that his uncle was in heaven. The other said that I was encouraging some guy named Henry to follow through. Yes, two very strong reactions. Again, I did a study and reasoned that if we don't earn our salvation by works, then we don't lose it by sin. If God is a gracious God, if he understands how dark and desperate a situation is, if he could have grace and compassion for this poor woman, then why can't we?"

I sensed his frustration regarding the split reaction from the members of his congregation.

"And how does this make you feel?" I asked.

"When we first discovered our son had died, there was so much darkness. Just an overwhelming darkness came upon us in waves, flooding our lives. People who knew me at the time later said that it had seemed like I was hunched over all the time, walking like I was carrying a burden. I remember arguing and pleading with God, 'Can I just take this heavy backpack off and lay it down for half an hour? Then I'll pick it up again. But just give me a half-hour!'"

I was taken aback by the guilt Russ had felt. It seemed so heavy. I wanted to help carry that weight for him, even if it was just for that half-hour he needed.

I started to choke up.

"In hindsight, why half an hour?" he continued. "Why not ask for a day? The answer is that when you feel so beaten up, all you can dare to ask for is a half-hour. I didn't have the courage or faith to ask for more. This weight felt so heavy that I couldn't even breathe. I couldn't sleep. I couldn't think clearly. I just had the wind taken out of my sails completely.

"I've contemplated this, and our son obviously was experiencing lots of pain. Suicide amplifies and multiplies that pain. His pain was amplified and spread out over hundreds of people, maybe thousands. So suicide actually multiplies it.

"Another thing I learned, spiritually, is something Jesus teaches: we use the opposite weapon to what's used against us. If someone curses you, you bless; if someone slaps you on the face, you turn the other cheek. The deal with suicide is shame and secrecy. The reaction is that if your family member commits suicide, you get stuck in that same cycle of shame and secrecy. When the police told me that it was suicide, my first thought was, 'How are we going to hide this?' Instantly I realized that if we tried to hide it, we would never heal. From that moment on, my wife and I decided that we were going to be as open and honest about it as we possibly could.

"So you use the opposite weapon. In suicide, it's about shame and secrecy. You don't let anybody know what you're going through, because if you let people know, you wouldn't be able to follow through. People would stop you. We determined to do the opposite—to talk about it openly. That's what made our healing possible. Or at least it's one of the things. If we'd been filled with shame and secretive about this, we'd still be screwed up today. Make sense?"

What a revelation, I thought.

"Sure," I replied. "What else would you like to share about the topic of suicide?"

"For survivors, if you've had your relative die by suicide, you can get into a pattern of beating yourself up for not seeing it and doing something. Those thoughts never lead you anywhere good. I'm not saying you should just stick your head in the sand and ignore what's going on, but it's important to recognize that there are no good answers to these what-ifs. The natural tendency is to get angry and start to blame others. But I needed my wife more at that time than ever before, and vice versa. We recognized that we couldn't blame each other.

"Everybody in this life has missed things. It would have been very easy to blame Brad's girlfriend, for example, but we recognized very early on that blaming her wouldn't lead us anywhere good. She had the right to break up with him. Even at the funeral, we assured her that this wasn't her fault."

What incredible mercy and grace, I thought to myself.

For some reason, I was surprised to hear that Brad's girlfriend had attended the funeral. I was blown away by how forgiveness had saved Russ's marriage and their collective sanity.

And so I asked my final question: "What would you like to know more about in terms of suicide?"

"After our son died, we didn't feel the need personally to get involved with suicide support groups. I'm not speaking negatively about people who do, but sometimes people get on a crusade to raise awareness. We didn't feel that was something we were looking for. We had good friends, and I did a lot of reading. I read probably ten books, most of them from a Christian perspective on suicide.

"This happened shortly after I had resigned from pastoring in Morden and our family was still very close to the people of that church. The church was thrown into turmoil by this and they had a fellow from a mental health centre come and talk. So we went and that was very helpful. But as for today, I don't know that I at this point feel that I need to know something more about the topic."

I was so grateful to have heard Russ's story. As I slowly stood and pushed out a small grin, I shook his hand.

"I want to thank you," I said. "I want to thank you for being transparent and honest. Thank you for your time and your testimony, especially of healing."

"You're welcome," he replied.

CHAPTER EIGHT
Confronting Shadows

AFTER MEETING WITH Pastor Russ, my life took a meaningful turn. I became a registered instructor for the Canadian Red Cross, eager to teach their newly developed workshop on psychological first aid. Demetre, too, joined me on this journey and together we embarked on a path to empower others.

Through the course of this training, I crossed paths with a retired paramedic who had about ten years of experience in the field. The toll of constant exposure to trauma, particularly teenage suicides, had left her emotionally scarred.

Serendipitously, she became my partner in the course. As we got to know each other's professions, I shared about my writing project. Although I asked if she would consider an interview, she politely declined, cautious of potential triggers for her PTSD. Instead she introduced me to her ex-boss, Ryan, who did agree to be interviewed.

On a chilly December 7, 2018, my family and I met Ryan at a cozy coffee shop in Winnipeg's Sage Creek neighborhood. Despite his youthful appearance, Ryan seemed weary from bearing the weight of his years in service.

As we picked up our coffees and settled at a table, I promptly turned on the recorder, eager to begin.

"Ryan, how often do people disclose to you that they're suicidal?"

"I'm in a pretty unique line of work, seeing people for sometimes twenty minutes, or sometimes a few hours at a time. I would say that somebody discloses that they want to commit suicide about once a week, if I averaged it out. It depends on where I'm working in the city, because every area is different. Some might have more elderly people, or more downtown people. Some less fortunate, others more."

Immediately I calculated in my head what that meant. He dealt with about fifty interventions per year.

"What is your protocol when someone discloses and how do you respond to a suicidal person?"

"Well, to be honest with you, it's quite unfortunate. The protocol for me in my profession is just to get them to a hospital. That's the extent of what we've been trained to do. We get them to somebody who knows how to deal with it."

"What are the biggest challenges your profession faces when it comes to suicide?"

"Paramedics have an inherent ability, or an inherent capacity, to help," Ryan said. "They want to help, but for paramedics and suicide, there's a lack of education that goes along with this. A lot of paramedics feel deflated due to a lack of ability to really help people."

"How effective is your profession at responding to people who are suicidal, or with those who are bereaved by suicide loss?"

"I don't think our profession is effective at all. And yet I can honestly say that it has improved over the last twenty years. Just being able to openly talk about it makes a difference. It's spoken about more prevalently now. But I think it's becoming obvious that there's a need for us to be more effective. The struggle now is trying to get groups of people together, and it is happening. Our paramedic profession has to get behind it, and I believe that the paramedics *want* to get behind it. It's a matter of asking, who can we work with to share stories and become more effective in the way we treat people?"

"How effective do you feel we are as a society?" I asked.

"In general, we're probably not doing very well with suicide over the past twenty years. But it's gradually becoming unavoidable because everybody is being touched by it. I believe there's a collective societal push for people to be more educated and speak freely on this subject. Society is definitely continuing to push to address this problem, either at the political level, the family level, or the friendship level. And it's not just the healthcare field that sees this. All professions need to realize that everyone is affected by it."

As he spoke, I could sense his discouragement. I could hear it in his voice.

"So what do you think we're doing wrong?"

"We still have a large stereotype out there as to who these people are who commit suicide and why they do it. I think we need to break down that stereotype, that barrier. We're not going to start healing people until we admit that we've got a major problem."

"What, in your opinion, could be done to improve how we deal with the problem of suicide?"

"I'm just taking a shot at this because I don't know the exact right answer," he acknowledged. "But in my field, I believe we need more readily available spaces where people can go to meet with counsellors, educators, and those who understand what it's like to feel suicidal and all that comes with it. We need real people to talk to. I believe that would make a strong, positive difference."

"And how big do you think the problem of suicide is?"

"I don't even know how big it is, but it's big. It may be way bigger than I think. I know it's not smaller than what I think."

"Has suicide impacted you in any way in your own life?"

"Suicide certainly impacts me on a professional level," he said. "As a paramedic, I work twelve-hour shifts for four days straight, and I meet someone contemplating suicide about once a week. There are times when I don't feel like I can help them, and sometimes it's a person who is very close to actually going through with it. That can bleed right into my personal life on my days off. You do sometimes catch yourself wondering, 'Did I help that person enough? Could I have helped them more? What can I do better next time?' So it certainly impacts me.

"Family-wise, I haven't necessarily been impacted. One cousin I didn't know that well took his life. He was addicted to fentanyl. My wife had a close family friend take his life and we've had a chance to talk about it, so I think that's a positive thing."

I leaned in. "Do you know any colleagues or people in your community who are at risk of suicide?"

"I certainly do know a couple of colleagues who have actually gone through with committing suicide," Ryan told me. "I also know of some who are currently dealing with that struggle. We're reaching out as a profession to try to catch these people. So I see it everywhere I go, but at different levels. It certainly affects me most at the professional level."

"How does this make you feel?"

"At times, like I said before, I feel deflated because I wish I could do more. But even though I'm a mentally strong and resilient person, I don't know whether every paramedic comes at it from the same way. As strong as anyone is, you can still be affected one time out of the clear blue. Some of my closest friends are strong-willed, strong mental personalities, and I've seen them go through some very tough mental challenges when it comes to calls at work. It has affected people I never would have thought it would affect, and they take time off work. This makes me think either I'm somewhat rare, or maybe something devastating might be coming around the corner for me."

"What else would you like to share about the topic of suicide?"

"To a lot of people, suicide is the final decision. The culmination of many small incidents that may have built up over time. For me, in my profession and the people I deal with as patients, it's so important to recognize the little things that slowly build up and can lead to suicide. It's important to identify these occupational stress injuries, or OSIs. They can accumulate and lead a paramedic to a place and they don't know how they got there. We should be self-aware about what is happening to our mental capacity and continually talk about it."

"When it comes to suicide, what would you like to know more about?"

"Well, to be honest, I think it would be important to recognize the stages of suicide, and the different outlets, personal and professional, for me and my colleagues. I'd like to know more about how the government is going to push forward to help our ever-changing population. The more we talk about suicide, the more we'll find out how prevalent it is. We need to know there's going to be a larger safety net so people don't slip through the cracks."

As the conversation had gone on, I'd grown quite fond of Ryan and admired his dedication to serving the public. What impressed me most was his genuine care for the people he worked with. Many individuals in public service face discouragement due to the lack of tools and resources available.

Unfortunately, Ryan couldn't benefit from the training I offered, as he couldn't afford to take two days off work. And he revealed that his colleagues and teammates were in the same situation due to being short-staffed.

At the end of the conversation, I stood up and shook his hand. I valued the time I'd spent with Ryan and respected his commitment to his family. I didn't want to impose on his time any further, but I expressed hope that one day soon I could provide training for his teammates.

CHAPTER NINE

Caring, Compassionate Community

A GOOD FRIEND of mine, Lorne Korol, holds the position of chaplain for both the Winnipeg Jets and the Winnipeg Blue Bombers. Knowing that Lorne was acquainted with Devon Clunis, a previous Winnipeg chief of police, I reached out to him. My intention was to gain insight into the prevalence of suicide on our streets and in our communities from a veteran officer.

After contacting Devon, it took a while to receive a reply. But we finally connected and arranged to speak over the phone.

"Hi, this is Devon here," he said when he answered.

I knew he was calling from a warm place and wanted to lighten the mood, so I made a point of talking about the weather. It was only -3°C that day.

Mr. Clunis laughed. "Not bad at all."

Unfortunately, we experienced some static and reception issues in the beginning, making it hard to hear each other clearly. But I persisted, and thankfully the connection improved.

"I really appreciate your time," I began. "For the book I'm writing, I'm speaking to people who are connected to the subject of suicide, and you are well-known in many of our communities here in Manitoba."

I went on to tell him about my passion and interest in the topic as a survivor. I also described my training, the ASIST model, and my recent participation with the Canadian Red Cross. The truth is that I couldn't think straight. I was trying so hard to establish my credibility when in reality I just needed to relax and let God remind me what I needed to ask.

"Let me start off with my first question. How often do people disclose to you that they're contemplating suicide, whether that was in your former job, or even today with people you come into contact with?"

"Well, not a lot of people today, considering the nature of my work in the consulting field. I'm usually going in and dealing with, you know, executives of organizations. In terms of interviews and the nature of my work with them, I don't have the opportunity for disclosures like that. But in the past, in terms of my regular police work, you can imagine the number of calls we were dispatched to about that. I've had a lot of unfortunate experiences in the past dealing with people who were threatening suicide, or sadly those who had successfully committed suicide.

"That was a piece of the training in the police organization. We had regular contact with people who were definitely suicidal. We needed the right training to be able to assist people in that situation. There were times when I would be, for example, on a bridge with somebody who wanted to commit suicide. Or I'd get into a hole with somebody who was holding a knife and wanted to commit suicide. It's just about being able to put yourself a little bit in their place, having a real, sincere empathy for them and recognizing that they've gone through traumatic pain that has brought them to this place.

"At some point in time, you realize that you truly are the lifeline in terms of making a difference in the world. I would challenge myself in those situations to say, 'Today you are going to make a significant difference.' We could actually go home knowing that our work that day had changed the course of someone's life. Every one of us has the opportunity to do that, whether we're in an official capacity or not.

"Suicide is really tragic. I've had very close friends, and members of my family, who have committed. So I've attended funerals like that. It probably hits close to home for most of us."

"Was that a problem in the police force as well? Were people at risk of suicide?"

"Well, absolutely. Think about people in emergency services, right? That's not just us in the police. But more police lose their lives to suicide than the number who get killed in the line of duty. A look at the facts will tell you that. During my tenure in the police service, we had a number of individuals who committed suicide. Some were very high-level. There were many suicides during my time in Winnipeg. I'm talking more than twenty-nine years as a police officer. Officers are not immune to this. If anything, because of the exposure and the type of work we're doing, we're more susceptible, because at the end of the day we're only human. I think people tend to forget that.

"We need to be able to have support mechanisms in place. Right now, when we look at where policing is going, one of the primary things is our need to do a much better job in terms of taking care of the mental wellbeing of our members—again, not just those in uniform but all the members of the emergency services organizations."

Hearing this really saddened me.

"What is your protocol when someone discloses?" I asked. "How do you respond to a suicidal person?"

"If you're speaking in terms of ourselves responding to someone in the community, we have really excellent training in that regard. We have all the right protocols and mechanisms in place to refer them to the right medical assistance. So in terms of being a police officer, we only have so much responsibility. We're not the ones providing the end care, but we get the person into the right system to provide that care.

"Within the organization, we truly have an excellent support system in place. We have our own police psychologist, and we have what we call wellness officers. Every member of the organization, particularly our supervisors, is trained to spot when something isn't right with our members. Let's say a member goes through what we would consider to be a traumatic incident. It's mandatory for them to then meet with the psychologist. The fact that we have made this mandatory really removes the stigma. In the past, people wouldn't want to seek psychological help on their own. If somebody went on their own, it would seem that they're 'less than.' Now that it's mandatory, everyone can hold their heads up and say, 'Well, you know what, the organization made me do it.' We've taken away the stigma.

"So we have a really good system in place within the Winnipeg Police Service, but also in many other police organizations. It's getting better all the time. In addition to the psychologist and wellness officers, we also have peer support groups. We really do recognize the importance of taking care of our members. We have strong protocols in place to ensure that their mental wellbeing is taken care of."

As I moved on to my next question, I felt so relieved to hear that. "What is the biggest challenge your profession faces when it comes to suicide?"

"I think the biggest challenge still is just the macho image of police work and those in emergency services work. People still need to get over seeing psychological challenges as being a weakness. They may ask themselves, 'Is this going to impact my career negatively?' So it's important that we get people past that mindset to recognize that, as human beings, most of us go through some type of mental health crisis. That doesn't mean we're less than anyone else. We have the same capabilities; it simply shows that we're human. We're getting to the point of normalizing the fact that a person in their lifetime may need some mental help.

"Consider what happens when we get injured in the line of duty and have to be off work—like, if we break a leg or an arm or something like that. We need to look at mental challenges very much the same way. You're going through a mental health crisis? Let's make sure that we take care of you the same way we take care of somebody with a physical injury. It's no different than if you broke your leg. So to me, that's the biggest challenge. I think we're overcoming the stigma, but we still have a long way to go for people to recognize that this isn't something for us to look at negatively.

"For me, when somebody comes forward and says, 'I'm having a challenge' or 'I need some help here,' I see that as a measure of strength. That's the type of person I want around me, because they're going to recognize their own need. They're also recognizing my need. And they won't be hesitant about reaching out to find the right help. That's the biggest thing we have to overcome."

I nodded along. "In your opinion, how effective is your profession at responding to people who are suicidal or who are bereaved by suicide loss?"

"Again, in terms of responding to people in crisis, we do an excellent job," Devon replied. "When somebody calls and they're in need, we put them in the right channels to get the right type of help for them. At the same time, I don't know if we have a robust enough support mechanism in place in the broader community. There are times when we encounter somebody who we think is experiencing some type of a mental health crisis. So we take them for the proper assessment in a hospital, but they get released. On occasion, they're released simply because we don't have enough of a support mechanism to take care of them. We can definitely do a better job so we don't see the same person back in another crisis a week or two later.

"Of all the police services across North America, Winnipeg has one of the best support systems. I know this for a fact. We have a plan in place and we do a very good job of educating the membership about why we do what we do, what it's for, and make sure there's no stigma attached to it. I feel very proud of the type of police organization we have in Winnipeg that takes very good care of our people but also takes exceptionally good care of the community in the context of policing.

"I can tell you that all of policing is moving very strongly in the direction of recognizing the great challenges of mental health issues in the community. We're all facing this. Police services are doing everything they can to prepare frontline members to respond appropriately. But within the community as a whole, we need to do a better job. When emergency workers bring a person in crisis to a medical facility, we need to have the capacity to treat and help them."

"How are the police responding to those who are bereaved by suicide loss?"

"Very compassionately," he said. "I'll speak specifically about Winnipeg. Let's talk about our victim services unit. We get in touch with families who have been bereaved, whether by suicide or any other type of significant trauma. We reach out to the community and we're certainly there to assist them. The same thing is true within the organization itself. When a family has experienced this, our people reach out to them and recognize the stigma that's attached to something like that. We try to break it down.

"The whole issue of mental health, of suicide, is something that society is becoming more aware of. But within emergency services, we're already very much aware. The strategic plan for the Winnipeg police has four pillars, and the wellness of the members is one of them. It's a foundational piece. In the United States, twenty-first-century policing has six pillars, and one of them definitely speaks to the wellness of the members of the organization. So the issue of mental health, the mental wellbeing of emergency service workers, is at the forefront of everything we're doing now."

"In your opinion, how effective is society in dealing with this issue? What are we doing right and what are we doing wrong?"

"I really don't think we're as effective as we should be. I talked earlier about destigmatization, and we're not doing enough on that front. I don't believe that we have enough resources in the community. We do a lot in terms of response, but we need to be proactive. We should be looking at why people are finding themselves in crisis. We need to have the science, the stats, the metrics behind why many people are so challenged. Then we can reduce some of those conditions that make us prone to crises. We can do a much better job.

"Yes, we're incredibly connected in terms of technology, but I think we've probably never been more disconnected in terms of understanding and caring for people on an emotional level. It's very difficult for me to feel your emotional care for me from just a text message, for example. If you and I are having a conversation electronically, just by the written word, I don't think it would be the same as hearing your voice. I couldn't hear the inflection of your care. That's one of the things we're doing poorly in society right now. We say we care, but caring takes time. So we need to slow down and actually get back to some of the face-to-face connections that ensure we're connected humanly, not just technologically.

"Those things we're not doing well. If we continue down this path and think technology is going to solve all our issues, we're wrong. It can solve many, but it will not replace human contact, which is what people are actually craving. That's what leads to a lot of the mental health challenges we're facing. We're human beings, and human beings need one another. We need to be connected. We need to remember, as we rush down the road of technology and advancement, that ultimately human beings need contact with others who say, 'I care about you.'"

Devon was bang-on. I felt that it's true: we're losing connection with one another, especially through texting. There are so many opportunities for misunderstanding when we're firing off quick replies without trying to understand the feelings behind each word.

For me, I find text messaging exhausting. You have to carefully read each word before you respond or risk getting into unnecessary trouble. And don't get me started with autocorrect. What a nuisance autocorrect can be!

"What can be done to improve how we deal with the problem of suicide?" I asked.

"I talked about it earlier, but I think the first thing we need to do is have more conversation about what's driving this. If we're going to do any studies, let's look at some of the root causes. Let's see if we have certain segments of the community who are more susceptible to this and start tackling those issues. At the same time, we must understand that we're dealing with people's desire for connection in a caring community.

"In policing, I talk a lot about leadership. Ultimately, here is what's most important. When leaders know they can make a mistake, because people understand that everyone makes them, they don't feel the same level of anxiety. They don't have to make sure everything's perfect. What we're looking for is caring, compassionate leaders who build caring, compassionate organizations that translate into caring, compassionate communities.

"Time and time again, when something negative occurs, whether it be within an organization or outside it, people are thrown to the wolves. But in my experience, I let people know that I'm there for them. I say, 'I expect that you're human and you will make a mistake.' Then something really incredible happens: you find that people make fewer mistakes. And when something negative happens, you can stand up and deal with it. It doesn't produce the same level of emotional stress and fatigue to the organization or the individual.

"There's a better way to go about this in terms of building up people, institutions, and organizations... ultimately, building up our society. That's a key thing we need to get back to. I think we're far too disconnected from that important, intrinsic human factor in everything we do. We can do much better. Even the fact that you're writing a book like this, that addresses some of these things, is important. I hope people read it because that's what we need to get back to. People aren't just numbers out there. We need to get back to the human factor, which makes such a significant difference."

"How big do you think the problem of suicide is?" I asked. "The World Health Organization has declared it a global crisis, and that every forty seconds in the world we lose someone to suicide. That's been reported."

"Well, I would not be surprised," Devon replied. "Just today, I saw something, a report that came down the wire. A U.K. doctor just said that men under fifty, I believe, are more likely to die from suicide than anything else. That's significant! Think about that for a second! We're talking about cancer, heart disease, and all these other illnesses... yet the number one killer of men who should be in the prime of their lives is suicide. They're the ones taking their lives. So I agree with you one hundred percent. We need to be talking about this and bring an awareness to what's driving it."

"And how does this make you feel, knowing that we're losing so many people, so frequently, in the world today?"

Devon answered right away. "Well, you know my mindset, in terms of how I feel. I look at the difference I can make. That's why I continue to work in the policing field, because I feel that policing is one of the more important institutions, bar none. Whether I was an officer or not, I would continue to try to make police organizations better, to have a stronger and more positive impact on communities.

"In terms of how it makes me feel, I've talked about the fact that we have to get people reconnected. I'm not one who gets easily dismayed when I see something that needs to be corrected. It just emboldens me to say, 'There's more for us to do.' It drives me to continue doing the kind of work I'm doing."

"What else would you like to share about this topic of suicide?"

"The topic of suicide impacts every single one of us. It's about the human factor, the human connection. That's something we really need to talk about. And it's something that every single one of us has: an ability to affect others in a positive way. We just need to know there's a role for us to play. We can make a significant difference with our smallest actions. Because you never know what someone is going through. It could be just a smile or a word that makes a difference in that person's day, something that turns them in a different direction from where they might have been headed."

I had only one question left for him. "What would you like to know more about in terms of suicide?"

"Well, I talked about it earlier, but I'd like to know specifically what some of the drivers are. We have the capacity to study this and ask about which specific groups are more prone. We need to look, for example, at immigrants or refugees in terms of the amount of stress they are going through. I'm saying we need to look at specific demographics and see from the stats who is being disproportionately affected. Sometimes we use a blanket solution and that's not always the best way to go. When we take actions, they need to be backed up by some science based on what we're seeing within our community. We could be far more targeted in our approaches, backed up by facts."

"Well, Devon, I want to thank you for your time. I know that your time is important to you and I want to respect that. I appreciate everything that you've shared."

"I appreciate you giving me the opportunity. Good luck with your book and we'll connect when I get back to town."

As I ended the call, I reflected on how inspiring it is to hear about the efforts and dedication put forth to ensure the safety of our police officers. They play a vital role in our communities. And while they're not perfect, like any of us, they are valued citizens who put their lives on the line to protect us.

Prayer is a powerful tool, and I pray for our police officers' well-being, especially when I witness them rushing into potentially dangerous situations with their lights flashing and sirens blaring. We all need to support and have each other's backs, fostering a sense of unity and collaboration.

It was evident that Devon's hard work and commitment continue to make a positive impact as he strives to create safe communities for everyone. We should appreciate and admire such efforts.

CHAPTER TEN

Emptiness, Hurt, and Anger

I HAVE KNOWN Mike Vogiatzakis for more than thirty years. Our fathers were very good friends.

After my father's funeral and burial, I went to visit Mike, who is the owner and funeral director of Voyage Funeral Home. I was curious to know whether he had noticed an increase in suicide rates among teenagers since he opened his business in the 1990s. My curiosity was personal, as I had struggled with suicidal thoughts when I was a teenager. I had a feeling that Mike would have some answers about the extent of the problem of teen suicides in Manitoba.

Mike brought me into a quiet conference room for the interview. He sat across from me with his hands folded, ready to talk.

"In your line of work, Mike, how often do people disclose that they're contemplating suicide?"

"I deal with many families and do a lot of arrangements. And during those arrangements, I'd say one out of every ten arrangements I do will involve suicide in one way or another. Whether it's a family member or a friend or somebody who was touched by the death, or prior to the death. So one out of ten families would talk about suicide."

This confirmed my instincts, but I also felt alarmed at how frequently he talked about suicide in his line of work.

"What is your protocol when someone discloses, and how do you respond to a suicidal person?"

"When I get a chance to be face-to-face with a suicidal person, I'll take all the precautions possible, putting them in touch with the right people, providing phone numbers, and going as far as taking them to the Health Sciences Centre crisis center. You need to deal with suicide in a very cautious manner, especially because you're dealing with death at the same time. I could share many stories about young people that I've done funerals for. Dealing with suicide is a very touchy subject and it becomes more touchy when the help is really not there for families."

"And what are the biggest challenges that your profession faces when it comes to suicide?"

"The biggest challenge we face as funeral directors, or people in the death industry in general, is not having places to send people that will take it seriously enough. We can send people to the Health Sciences Centre, for example, and a doctor will assess them. But sometimes those don't last very long. If the patient doesn't want to stay, he just puts on a pretty face and manages to walk out five minutes later.

"So dealing with suicide in the city of Winnipeg and the province of Manitoba is a difficult situation. We definitely need more resources. We need more literature. We need more people we can contact right now who will take action immediately instead of phoning a suicide hotline. When somebody reaches out and wants to commit suicide, you need to talk right now. Not tomorrow, not next week. Now, when everything is right there on the table."

"In your opinion, how effective is your profession at responding to people who are suicidal, or people who are bereaved by suicide loss?"

"In my profession, I don't think a lot of people would deal with suicide," Mike said. "They would deal with making the funeral arrangements and possibly brush off the thought of suicide. So I think it becomes the responsibility of a director who has the right heart, a director who believes, a director who cares to take action and maybe stop a suicide or get help for that person. They could even talk to them, maybe say a prayer for them, or just spend some time. When somebody's wanting to commit suicide, or talking about suicide, a lot of times they're talking out loud. They're screaming for help. As a funeral director, when somebody's screaming for help, I'm not doing them any justice if I don't have the time to give them that help. So it takes a special person to sit and spend as much time talking as the person needs. We need to say, 'What can I do to help? What's bothering you? How can we fix this problem?' But of course we're not trained professionals in suicide; we're trained in the death industry. We take counseling courses, but the bottom line is we need the right resources to make that connection."

"How effective do you feel society is at dealing with suicide? What are we doing right and what are we doing wrong?"

"Suicide is a tough subject to talk about, between mental illness and addictions, and a lot of it is pushed aside and not dealt with properly. I think that's why there's an outbreak of suicides. Right now, during COVID lockdowns, some of the decisions the government makes relating to isolation is driving people to the tumultuous side. The last thing you want to do with somebody who's suicidal is leave them alone to think about what they want to do. And a person who's willing to commit suicide has been in a dark place for quite a while.

"Society really needs to come to grips with suicide. We need to come to grips with mental illness. And we need more resources and more help, because when somebody wants to commit suicide, it's not something that just happens. It's a thought they've had for a while. They're in a very, very dark place and can't see the light. That's when suicide takes place. We need to make sure that the light shines upon them to give them hope."

"What could we do to improve how we deal with the problem of suicide?"

"In my opinion, having more resources available would make a big difference. We should have centers that take this seriously, with intake workers who are going to spend time with people. I also think when someone is assessed, they should be kept for a mandatory forty-eight hours so the professionals can do what they need to do and talk with them and find out where their hearts are at. For every minute we spend with somebody who's going to commit suicide, it's a minute spent saving a life. We really need to change the way they deal with this.

"For example, when you have somebody with cancer, there's cancer care available. When you have somebody with heart disease, there are hospitals that deal with heart disease. But there's really not a specific place that deals with mental health and suicide. There are prevention lines. People do try to take part, but we need to more than take part. We need action—action that happens right now, when we find out that somebody is on the verge of committing suicide. Or maybe they're screaming that out.

"I have a neighbor who is a police officer and he says the same thing. They pick up somebody who's going to commit suicide, and a few hours later that person is back on the street again. Sometimes a few hours later, they're dead."

As I listened, I felt impressed. This man had been deeply impacted by suicide. He had carefully thought through a lot of these thoughts. So far the interview was going into places that I hadn't anticipated.

I moved forward to my next question. "How big do you think the suicide crisis is in Manitoba and the rest of the world?"

"I think the suicide crisis is huge. As a matter of fact, since COVID-19, we've been dealing with an outbreak of suicides at the funeral home, more suicides than I've ever probably done as a funeral director in twenty-one years. People are depressed. People are angry. People are walking around with anxiety. The pressures of the world are getting to people. COVID-19 has put more pressure on families with unemployment and people are losing hope in tomorrow. They don't have money in their pockets. They're unable to pay the rent or put food on the table. It's a huge crisis right now, and it's not just a Canadian crisis. It's a crisis right across the world."

"What if I were to tell you that the World Health Organization has reported that suicide is a global crisis and that we're losing one person to it every forty seconds?"

"I would truly believe that. From the number of suicide deaths at the funeral home, it is a global crisis. I've talked with funeral directors around the world, and they're saying the same thing—that suicides are on the rise and nothing is being done about it. We're talking about somebody's life. Somebody's kid. Somebody's mom. Somebody's daughter. We need to take people's lives seriously.

"It's serious to call this a global crisis, and we need to take serious action. Our governments need to come together and realize that lives are being lost because they're not doing anything about it. We need to put pressure on the government to open up facilities to deal with suicide and mental illness in a new way, and not just talk about it."

"Has suicide impacted you in any way in your own life?"

"Yes. A suicide once impacted my wife's family. One of her uncles committed suicide. It's a terrible feeling of emptiness and loneliness. You think, 'What if I could have done something?' All those thoughts come into your mind.

"As a funeral director, I've dealt with suicide on a personal level with younger people who come through the funeral home with their families. Shortly after, I hear that this same young gentleman, who was sitting at my table making arrangements for his grandpa, has now committed suicide. It's hurtful because there was nothing I could do about it. There is no way to help this person. No way to even know about it. I think people need to be more open. Family members need to be open. When the word *suicide* comes from a person's mouth, that needs to be dealt with. That's a cry for help.

"And just recently, a funeral director who worked for me for many years ended up committing suicide. He was dealing with addiction. In fact, that just happened two weeks ago and it's left an emptiness in my own heart. I keep wondering, 'Hey, is he going to send me something in the mail to tell me that he was going to do this?' In our last conversation, I filled his heart with hope and told him to have faith, for tomorrow would be a new day—and he ended up killing himself. It's shocking to hear that news, that a friend you've known very well has taken his life. It just fills you with emptiness and you wonder why you didn't do more to help."

Mike's heart was sincere. I could sense it in his voice and in his attitude.

I carried on. "And how have you dealt with those feelings?"

"One thing I've learned to do as a funeral director, and I've taught myself to do this, is to leave my work at work and to go home and be with my family. Deep in my heart, suicide touches me in a drastic way. When I have to do arrangements for a young gentleman or a young father who has committed suicide, it's devastating to deal with. You're dealing with emptiness, hurt, and anger, and there's nothing you can do about it. You need to leave your work and go talk to your own family. I have a son and I talk with him constantly to make sure his heart and mind are in the right place. I ask him a lot of questions about things that are bothering him—"

Right at that moment, in the middle of the interview, my phone rang and I couldn't turn down the volume. It was highly inconvenient, to say it least.

I ignored the call, regained my focus, and continued. "What else would you like to share about the topic of suicide?"

"I just wish, as a funeral director, that the world would care more, and that we would show more love and pay attention to people. We should realize that people are hurting in this world and lacking love and attention. They're not getting the support they need from their parents, and there's no real support in schools to help those who want to commit suicide. The world is reaching out and asking for help, and we need to put people in touch with them who will do that, who will take them seriously. Whatever we do in this world, if we're struggling, I worry that we're just another statistic.

"My personal opinion is that more people need to know God. I think Jesus plays a big part in our hearts and souls. People need to know that there's forgiveness if they've done something wrong, that tomorrow's a new day. It's like taking a white sheet that's completely dirty and throwing it in the laundry, and it comes out crispy white. That's forgiveness.

"I think the world has caused a lot of hurt. For kids, it starts at a very young age. They take the Lord's prayer out of school, they take away Bibles, and they take away our hope in believing in something. As a funeral director, I wish we could have more in our lives, because we need that. I talk about this often, that it doesn't matter what you have in life, everything is on a lease and nothing is really yours. So don't stress about the things you lose or the things you can't have, because you can't take anything with you at the end.

"Education is a big part of suicide too. I'm talking about education on how to get help and education on how to move on. Let's get people attached to a good church that provides a good ministry and has people who can help. When you're dealing with a suicide crisis, it's important to surround yourself with positive people. You are who you hang out with. If you have friends who are doing drugs, eventually you're going to do drugs. And if you have friends who are alcoholics, eventually you're going to start drinking. But if you have friends who have the right thoughts and are trying to get high on life, that'll take you to the next level. People need to be inspired. We need more hope and faith in this world."

I felt like I was hearing a great sermon, and because of it I began to feel encouraged and inspired. For a moment, I thought that Mike might have missed his calling to be a pastor.

"And what would you like to know more about in terms of suicide?"

"The topic of suicide is so unknown. We don't know what really triggers suicide and what people's thoughts are. I think we need to be better educated on the triggers. What are the real views of suicide, and how should we deal with suicide victims or patients or clients? The bottom line is that we need more education. We need to get deeper into this and know the professionals who are on the front lines. They can tell us how serious the threat is, what the triggers are, what the cries are, and how we can help as leadership professionals."

I smiled and stood up, expressing my gratitude. "Well, Mike, that was my last question. Thank you very much. This interview has been inspirational, and I really want to thank you for your time."

"Thank you, Billy," Mike replied warmly. "Keep doing your good work."

With a sense of fulfillment and newfound understanding, I left the conference room, knowing that the conversation had shed light on important issues. I felt encouraged to continue my efforts in raising awareness and supporting those in need.

But I felt my internal wellbeing becoming increasingly affected by all the interviews I'd conducted over the previous three years. I pretended to be strong, but inside I was falling apart.

CHAPTER ELEVEN
Looking for Attention

AFTER MY INTERVIEW with Mike Vogiatzakis in November 2020, I started to slip into depression. To cope with the grief of losing my father on September 6, 2020, I resorted to unhealthy eating habits, consuming a lot of fast food, snacks, sugary drinks, and coffee. Over time, this led to a significant weight gain. I reached close to three hundred pounds and had various physical discomforts and interrupted sleep patterns.

Trudy grew concerned about my fear of going to the hospital due to being unvaccinated for COVID-19. I had chosen not to get the shot until more data came out, since I felt overwhelmed by conflicting reports.

Eventually I visited a homeopathic doctor, but his advice didn't resonate with me and I felt anxious during the visit. I briefly tried some natural detox medicines but gave up on them.

During the lockdowns of 2020, I'd lost my job as a manager in the human services field, a role I'd held for nearly eight years. I decided to become a licensed realtor but faced vaccine mandates when trying to take the licensing exam. I refused to comply, which made it difficult to find new opportunities. My family and friends were divided on their view of the vaccine, and gathering restrictions and church closures intensified the strain. Trudy and I considered renting our home due to the financial pressure, but we couldn't find the right tenants.

All this stress took a toll on my health and I fell seriously ill in December 2022. While having a nightmare about drowning, which I wrote about in this book's introduction, I had a near-death experience and woke up gasping for air. I felt so isolated and frightened. In that moment, I realized that I wanted to live and cherish my time with Trudy. I also wanted to see our family grow so we could explore the world together.

Depression is a gradual process, and it didn't happen overnight in my case. But sitting down in front of my laptop on the night of my nightmare gave me hope and motivation to complete this book, a project which I had allowed to languish. The incredible stories I had gathered deserved to be heard and honored.

In 2017, I taught a workshop at the public library in Steinbach, Manitoba. One of the participants had been Yael Fehr, a high school guidance counselor at the time. We developed a friendship after the workshop and I also got to know her husband Peter and their three children. Peter and I became close friends over the years.

Five years later, in December 2022, I felt compelled to reach out to Yael and ask her to share some of her experiences as a counselor, particularly regarding the problem of suicide in schools. Due to the short notice, though, I had to send her the questions via email.

Yael's response was heartfelt and insightful.

"In a high school, it was not uncommon to hear suicidal ideation daily," she replied to me in writing. "Sometimes all that was needed was a caring listener to change that. In the time I worked there, I took three students to the hospital, but I also spoke to a few parents and had them hear their kids and care for them after disclosure.

"I was one of three staff trained in ASIST and concerned teachers and staff brought me many students. Sometimes I listened to their stories, and that was all they needed. If the concern was suicide, I reached out to another ASIST-trained staff person to help me keep the student safe until a plan could be put in place. As I said, sometimes that meant having a parent come in and assume care for the students. If there was concern that the parents weren't safe, then the student would be brought to the mental health practitioner at the hospital.

"I think one of the biggest challenges might be the attitude that the students were just looking for attention. If they really wanted to do it, they wouldn't talk about it. The thing is, they *were* talking, often to other youth who aren't meant to be responsible in dealing with suicide because they have a sympathetic ear.

"I also think some teachers hear this talk and question whether it's serious. There are some teachers and staff in every school who are authentically there for the betterment of their students, and they are effective, but not all are like that. That's a concern.

"I think society is similar to individual institutions. Some get that this is a serious concern for all age groups, and others do not. Big steps have recently been taken in the area of mental health and illness. However, I know of a person who was suicidal and acting on it, and the people responsible for her merely got angry and refused to help the way she needed. They held her in lockup for hours, promising appropriate care, and then just sent her home. Not good.

"There is support available for those caught in mental illness, but not for those people's families. We need to provide families with a place to walk this journey with others who have gone through it, so they can find the supports they need for their at-risk person, as well as for themselves. You can't walk this alone. Everyone needs help.

"Education needs to happen. If there are still people out there who think a person only acts suicidal to get attention, then we fail. Suicide is a serious problem, and it's only getting worse with the added stress of a broken world that no longer gives us downtime.

"I most certainly have been impacted by suicide attempts and death. Not only myself, but my children, extended family, students, colleagues, and friends. A colleague committed suicide just last month. It's the hardest thing. It's draining and intensely emotional. I continue to walk the journey of that pain, and I do so in many ways.

"When it comes to suicide, I know too much. I wish I knew less. But there are so many who don't have the help they need, so I continue to be present. One thing I'm wondering about is how to set up a support system for people who are walking this.

"I don't have a lot of time, so these are quick answers. I think you might already know my thoughts on suicide and how important it is that we talk about it, and anything connected to it, a lot more."

I truly appreciated Yael's candid and informative response. Her experiences and dedication to addressing suicide and mental health issues are commendable. Her care and support for those going through difficult times have undoubtedly made a significant impact on people's lives.

CHAPTER TWELVE

i Will Not Be a Bystander

IN 2012, I worked for an organization supporting adults with fetal alcohol spectrum disorders and intellectual challenges. During that time, I shared with a coworker about the childhood memory of my brother and cousin almost drowning at a beach thirty years earlier.

He responded with a haunting tale of his own, recounting a day at the St. Malo beach. He noticed two teenagers crying and struggling to breathe in the water, and without hesitation he ran down the beach and dove in, determined to help them. But as he swam closer, he faced a gut-wrenching dilemma—which one would he save? Time was slipping away and he had to make a split-second decision.

Tragically, one of the girls went under the water and drowned before he could reach her.

His heart broke as he continued swimming towards the other girl, who was still fighting to stay afloat. He managed to reach her and dogpaddled with all his strength to get her safely to shore. Once on the beach, knowing that every second mattered, he immediately started performing CPR, hoping to revive her. For nearly thirty minutes, he gave it his all until the ambulance finally arrived.

Despite his efforts, the girl passed away.

He couldn't hold back his emotions while sharing this heart-wrenching story with me.

"How can a person live with something like that?" I asked.

"Honestly, I knew the odds were against me from the beginning," he replied. "There's only a ten percent chance of saving someone who's drowning. But I don't regret trying. I can live with myself, knowing that I did everything I could to save them. What I couldn't bear was the thought of being a mere bystander, watching those girls struggle without stepping in to help. There were so many people on the beach that day, but no one reached out or swam towards them until I did. Even when I got one of the girls to the beach, I had to direct someone to call 911 for an ambulance. It was as if people were paralyzed by fear or uncertainty. It's something I can't fathom. I can't live with the idea of just watching and doing nothing when lives are at stake. So, yes, I can live with myself for trying, even though the odds were stacked against us. But being a bystander? That's something I couldn't bear. You know what I mean?"

As he finished, his eyes glistened with unshed tears. His bravery and determination to make a difference were awe-inspiring. His story has made a profound impact on me till this day.

But fear gripped me and I couldn't help but pray, "God, please grant me the strength to act if I'm ever faced with such a situation." I felt overwhelmed by the weight of responsibility I would feel, and the knowledge that lives may hang in the balance.

I had observed that this coworker of mine always had a worn-out look on his face, and until now I had always wondered about the burdens he carried. It seemed evident to me that life had thrown numerous challenges his way.

Seven years later, I decided to share his powerful story at one of my speaking engagements in Steinbach. As I recounted the events of the man's fateful day at St. Malo beach, the room fell silent. The listeners' emotions ran high and tears were shed as the impact of his actions resonated.

After sharing the story, I gave the group a much-needed coffee break to process the intensity of the moment.

As people dispersed, a tall young woman approached me and revealed that the brave man I had talked about was her father. She had made the connection through my workplace and knew that her dad had shared this haunting experience with me.

Her father had kept a newspaper article about the incident, carefully taped behind his bedroom closet. She shared how he would occasionally stare at the article, still deeply affected by that tragic day. She thanked me for sharing his story, acknowledging its importance and the impact it had on others.

Her heartfelt gratitude reaffirmed my belief in the power of sharing experiences and stories, even if they're painful. It was a reminder that we can all make a difference and leave a lasting imprint on those around us.

After the young woman left, I felt stunned. It hit me that my own brother and Demetre's brother had been spared by God on that fateful day at Birds Hill Park. I couldn't bear the thought of what life could have been like without the two Georges, and I knew this story needed to be shared openly.

I arranged a meeting at a Winnipeg restaurant with Demetre and both Georges. As we sat down for coffee, my cousin began to share what happened that day.

He recalled that it had been the summer of 1978, when he was just seven years old. As families gathered at the beach, the two Georges had decided to go catch minnows. They took the swamp route, which turned out to leave them neck-deep in sticky mud. After finishing there, they chose the beach route to head back, hoping they could wade across when the water was deep enough.

However, as they stepped into the water, they found themselves on a steep slope, in over their heads. They started hopping to stay above the water, trying to call for help. But with each hop, they took in more water than air. Panic set in as they struggled to breathe and my cousin George realized he was drowning and wouldn't make it.

In the midst of this terrifying ordeal, a hero emerged. A teenage girl's arm reached in and pulled him to the surface, saving him from certain death.

Demetre and the girl saved the boys' lives. The shock of the experience left my cousin speechless for the entire drive home.

As I listened to his distressing account, my eyes welled up. It had taken forty-five years for me to hear the full story, and the emotions overwhelmed me. I was so grateful that they were still here, alive and well. It was undoubtedly a miracle. I thanked Jesus for their lives being spared.

This incident, along with all the other experiences I've encountered, made me realize that I've been a first responder since I was eight years old, hollering and pointing out crisis scenes. And that's what I'm still doing today through writing this book.

But I can't do it alone. Just like that eight-year-old boy did back in 1978 at Birds Hill Park, I need help.

To address the global health crisis of suicide, we need to take a village approach. Everyone must become a lifeguard in their homes, workplaces, communities, churches, and schools. We must help those facing mental health challenges and suicidal thoughts.

I'm reaching out for help, for heroes who will spread the word about suicide first aid training in their communities. We also need champions to fund these workshops, making them accessible to all, so more people can get involved in this vital mission.

This is my cry for help, and I'm not ashamed to say that I need everyone's support and commitment to make a difference.

CONCLUSION
God Keep Our Land

ON DECEMBER 23, 2022, I saw a Canadian company advertising medical aid in dying. The commercial showed a young woman struggling with financial debts. In summary, the message was that you could just end your life instead.

Oh Canada, I thought. *What have you become since Mr. Trudeau fulfilled his euthanasia campaign promise in 2016?*

When I was eighteen years old in May 1988, I survived my suicide attempt. Like the young woman in the commercial, I was struggling with thoughts of suicide. In my teenage years, I developed a narrative that my dad didn't care about me. He was a workaholic who had turned to alcohol, and I couldn't decide whether I hated him more for neglecting me or for his mean and abusive behavior.

I craved his guidance and support during my teenage years, but all I received was silence and criticism. He often spoke harshly and cursed at me, telling me I wouldn't amount to anything. I resented him deeply and rebelled against him in every way possible. It seemed the only time he paid attention to me was when I got into trouble, either at school or with the police.

One day, the situation reached a breaking point when my girlfriend and I broke up, and my dad made fun of me for it. Fueled by rage and hurt, I confronted him, and it escalated into a physical altercation. My physical strength surpassed his by this time and I was no longer afraid of him. He grabbed a shovel and swung it at me, but I managed to evade it. The fight continued until I had him pinned down, and for a moment I felt a sense of control and revenge.[2]

However, the gravity of my actions hit me at once. I felt like a cold-hearted monster.

How can anyone beat up their own father? I wondered over and over, tormenting myself.

My father got up and left the house, leaving me alone. I ran upstairs to the bathroom, took a razor blade, and started slashing my wrists. Each slash burned, but it couldn't take away the pain in my heart. I wanted to die. I was tired of being a loser and a burden to my family and everyone around me.

Somehow an image of my mother crying appeared to me and the spell of suicide immediately died. When I thought of my mom crying, I knew that my death would devastate her, so I panicked and turned towards saving my own life. I realized that I wanted to live.

In desperation, I saved myself by putting my wrists under cold water and wrapping towels around them. I called a friend for help and they picked me up and brought me to the emergency room at the Health Sciences Centre.

At the hospital, the triage nurse was puzzled as she didn't find any serious marks or deep cuts on my wrists. My friend's mom, a nurse, ensured that I received prompt attention, but I couldn't bring myself to cooperate with the doctor's inquiries. This doctor brought a team of resident students into my room and bombarded me with

[2] This entire story can be read in my previous book, *Following the Fire.*

questions. I completely shut down, feeling humiliated and embarrassed. I wasn't going to be their guinea pig.

With tears in my eyes, I looked away.

The doctor's voice didn't demonstrate care or empathy, nor did his questions. He went through his checklist and ignored me. As a patient that day, I suffered in silence.

Once the doctor and his team left the room, I managed to escape the hospital, feeling numb and conflicted.

Later I went to my aunt and uncle's home and explained what had happened. That's when my mother called, and I reluctantly agreed to see my dad at the psychiatric hospital—but I couldn't figure out why he was in such a facility.

I had to buzz in for the hospital to admit me. And when I arrived at my dad's floor, the elevator doors opened and I saw him nearby. I was shocked at the damage I had inflicted on him. He walked towards me, severely bruised and tearful. Then he hugged me and apologized for our fight.

Unable to handle the emotional turmoil, I left without reconciling with him.

In the following years, my relationship with my dad deteriorated further. I called him by his English name, Andy, to mock and distance myself from him. This deep hatred and denial led me to make poor choices and get into trouble.

At the age of thirty-one, I had a near-death experience that made me realize I needed to find God and seek his guidance to overcome life's challenges. In 2001, I made amends with my dad and asked for his forgiveness. Though we still had arguments, as all humans do, we always worked things out. I stopped disrespecting him and started calling him Dad again.

Since then, we talked almost every day and had a much-improved relationship. I even named my firstborn son, Andreas, in his honor. I cherished the time we spent together until his passing in 2020. I miss him deeply and am grateful for the chance to have resolved our issues and shared love and understanding. I know we will be reunited one day, both of us unbroken and at peace.

I'm incredibly grateful that MAiD wasn't available in 1988. In my rage and despair, I would have gladly chosen the option to die without a second thought during a hospital assessment. I firmly believe that governments and politicians should reconsider the implications of MAiD on citizens struggling with mental health issues.

Life itself is a fundamental truth, and we all face the certainty of death eventually. We don't need this inevitable truth to be hastened by interventions like MAiD. Just as capital punishment isn't a solution to cope with the losses caused by convicted criminals, MAiD should not be viewed as a solution to life's struggles.

I once had a conversation with a military policeman who shared an interesting observation. While he had to charge those who harmed others, no charges are ever brought against those who attempt suicide. It raises the question of whether there is a crime in such situations.

Over the years, I've pondered this and reflected on what Pastor Toews shared with me about suicide and salvation. I agree that salvation is a gift, just as life is.

In this hurting world, we need a Savior. I don't believe any government or person can save us, nor can we save ourselves. For me, that Savior is Jesus Christ. The text of John 3:16 always stands out, reminding us that through belief in him we can have eternal life.

Everyone deserves hope, and it's crucial to convey to those who struggle that they aren't burdens. They are not alone. The young woman in the commercial I saw needed to know that her life was precious and that help was available. We need to break the spell of suicide that falsely suggests that death is the answer to pain and suffering.

Those facing life's challenges need to understand that their absence would leave a significant void in the lives of others. That void never fades for the loved ones left behind. Amidst the busyness of life, we must make time to listen, understand, and lend a helping hand. Each of us has a unique story and purpose, and with God all things are possible.

Imagine the impact we could make if we all came together to love and support one another. We have the power to make a difference in the lives of those in need, to be beacons of hope and compassion and remind them that they aren't alone.

I believe we all have the power to make a difference. Just consider what would happen if we chose not to help others in their times of need. It would be like being in that cold, dark lake I wrote about at the beginning of the book, feeling isolated and frightened, unable to see those who care about us on the shore, ready to offer love and help.

We may not fully understand how we ended up in such a lonely and terrifying place, with unseen dangers lurking beneath the surface, but we'll find hope if we keep our eyes above the water. By looking up and crying out to Jesus, he will come to us in our despair and offer his help and love. Always remember to look up, for your Savior is closer than you might think.

May God continue to bless our land, keeping it glorious and free, as we come together to support and uplift one another in times of need.

AFTERWORD

AFTER I HAD that nightmare in December 2022, I took charge of my physical, mental, and spiritual health. This was a turning point for me. As I embarked on a journey to transform my life, I made significant changes, adopting a new healthy lifestyle that has had a positive impact on every aspect of my being.

I also focus on improving my relationship with God, my family, my friendships, and folks in my community. I focus on my physical health through regular exercise, eating a clean diet, and prioritizing self-care. As a result, I've lost a considerable amount of weight and feel more energetic and vibrant than ever before.

In addition to taking care of my body, I have also worked on nurturing my mental health. I have sought the support of the Holy Spirit, who reveals all truths to those who desire it. The Holy Spirit provides guidance, teaching us how to cope with stress. He challenges us in healthier ways. This has brought clarity and peace of mind, allowing me to approach life with a renewed sense of purpose and optimism.

Moreover, my spiritual health has become a central aspect of my journey. I've found solace and strength in my faith, deepening my connection with God. This newfound spiritual resilience has been a guiding light for me during difficult times and given me the courage to face life's uncertainties with hope and trust.

This transformative process has been life-changing, and I'm grateful for the growth and healing I've experienced. I'm now eagerly working on my next book, in which I'll share more about my journey to inspire and empower others to embrace their own path of healing and self-discovery. Stay tuned for *Back to the Land*. I hope it will offer insight and encouragement for those seeking to embark on their own transformative journeys to better their health and well-being.

ALSO BY BILL VASSILOPOULOS

Following the Fire

ISBN: 978-1-4866-1545-2

BILL SEEMS TO have a thing about fire. From setting a fire in a hollow tree stump as a child visiting his grandparents in Greece, to taking the heat from a bully, and getting burned by a drug deal gone bad, Bill goes from one hot spot to another. Follow the trail of fire as Bill tells of growing up in a traditional Greek family transplanted to Canada, and feeling the searing pain of his father's disappointment. But his burning desire to find God is not easily quenched. Now a new passion flames, and Bill invites his readers to join him as he follows the fire.

www.ingramcontent.com/pod-product-compliance
Lightning Source LLC
LaVergne TN
LVHW010624100826
845148LV00014B/3090

* 9 7 8 1 4 8 6 6 1 6 2 4 4 *